MONEY MAGIC TRICKS

BOB LONGE

Sterling Publishing Co., Inc.
New York

Library of Congress Cataloging-in-Publication Data
Longe, Bob, 1928-
   Money magic tricks / Bob Longe.
      p. cm.
   Includes index.
   ISBN 0-8069-8019-2
      1. Coin tricks. 2. Magic tricks. I. Title.

GV1559. L63 2001
793.8-dc21   2001034849

4   6   8   10   9   7   5

Published by Sterling Publishing Co., Inc.
387 Park Avenue South, New York, N.Y. 10016
© 2001 by Bob Longe
Distributed in Canada by Sterling Publishing
c/o Canadian Manda Group, 165 Dufferin Street,
Toronto, Ontario, Canada M6K 3H6
Distributed in the United Kingdom by GMC Distribution Services,
Castle Place, 166 High Street, Lewes, East Sussex, England BN7 1XU
Distributed in Australia by Capricorn Link (Australia) Pty. Ltd.
P.O. Box 704, Windsor, NSW 2756 Australia
Manufactured in the United States of America

Sterling ISBN-13: 978-0-8069-8019-5
ISBN-10: 0-8069-8019-2

For information about custom editions, special sales, premium and
corporate purchases, please contact Sterling Special Sales
Department at 800-805-5489 or specialsales@sterlingpub.com.

Contents

Introduction

Magic tricks with money? Right. What could be more convenient? Surely someone in the group has some coins or bills. On a good day, it might even be you.

And what superb tricks we have here! (I'm not being immodest; many others have made contributions.) There are over 60 tricks in all, ranging from extremely easy to fairly difficult. If you want to learn several simple tricks with which to amuse friends, you'll find them here. Or you might choose advanced tricks that will dazzle onlookers and impress them with your professionalism.

In either instance, you'll find tricks of every type here. Coins appear, disappear, change places, hop about under cards, and perform in many other peculiar ways.

You'll also learn a number of slick stunts with bills. Furthermore, you'll master several funny money tricks and many intriguing bets, challenges, and puzzles—all involved with money.

Every trick is clearly explained, and the book abounds with illustrations. What's more, you're given fascinating patter ideas for each trick. To cap it all, you're told how you might combine various tricks to form coherent routines; nothing is more professional than a series of tricks that seem to naturally blend together.

Perhaps the most significant section is "Secrets of Money Magic," in which you learn what makes these tricks work.

Bob Longe

Secrets of Money Magic

Some of the suggestions in this section are obvious; many more of them are subtle. Regardless, you'll find the real secrets to a successful performance.

Let me start with an anecdote. A few years ago I was at a restaurant where a variety of magicians from the Detroit area gathered on Monday nights. One out-of-town visitor was a young New Yorker who was proud of his sleight-of-hand ability. After watching him perform several tricks, I asked him, "Have you heard of Milt Kort?"

Since Kort's name appears in about every other book on magic, I felt I knew the answer.

"Certainly."

"Come along with me, I'll introduce you to him."

The young man followed me to the table where Milt sat with his daughter, superb illustrator Sandra Kort. I'd better tell you that Milt's name appears in so many professional magic books because he is not only a leading authority on magic, but is also one of the greatest close-up performers of all time.

The young performer said, "Want to see some coin tricks?"

"Sure," Milt said.

The young man removed several coins from his pocket and began bouncing them from hand to hand. Apparently some were disappearing, some were magically vanishing from one hand and appearing in the other, and some were just bouncing. It was hard to tell what he was doing.

"Slow down," said Milt.

But he did not slow down. He continued springing the coins about.

"Slow down," said Milt.

It didn't work. Milt shrugged and began conversing with his daughter. The young man strolled away to perform his sleight-of-hand miracles for a more appreciative audience. He had just received the best advice he'd ever get, and from one of the best-qualified persons in the world to give the advice. He's probably still doing tricky maneuvers for persons who are astonished, largely because they have no idea of what he's doing.

Let me give you Milt's advice: Slow down!

Give everyone a chance to understand what you're doing. Rarely is a sleight dependent on speed; the key is smoothness. You're a magician, not a juggler. Perform your sleights at a *natural* speed. Suppose, for instance, you have a coin in your right hand and are pretending to put it into your left hand. As you'll soon discover, there are several clever ways to accomplish this. But not one of them will be effective unless you make the sleight duplicate *exactly* the actual transfer of a coin. The movement should be neither too fast nor too slow; it should mimic the natural movement.

So, first place the coin in your left hand. Then perform the sleight. Keep alternating like this until the sleight feels as natural as the legitimate move. From time to time, check both movements in the mirror.

Practice *any* trick until it's second nature. This gives you confidence and allows you to concentrate on other aspects of your performance—your patter, for instance. Also, it gives you an opportunity to gauge your audience. Are they hanging on every word? Or should you pick up the pace? Perhaps you should go to the A-material. Maybe it's almost time to end the performance.

Please don't assume from the above that I'm suggesting that you work in slow motion. Far from it. Move right along, but make sure that everyone knows what your intentions are.

Furthermore, it's important that you don't waste time. How do you waste time? By wondering what you ought to do next. By inventing complicated story patter that makes no sense whatever. By aimlessly conversing with individual spectators. By telling jokes that don't relate at all to anything magical.

What else wastes time? Describing what you're doing while you're doing it. Here's a bit of news: *Everyone can see what you're doing!* Talk about something else. Stick to your patter theme, whatever it might be. But don't say, "Now I pick up the coin. Notice that I'm putting it into my left hand." This kind of monologue is poisonous, particularly when you're actually *not* putting the coin into your left hand. Why in the world would you want to call everyone's attention to a place where you don't really want it?

You've probably heard this many times, but it bears repeating: Don't tell your audience what you're going to do. That's it. If they know what you're going to do, they might just know where to look and *how* to look. Just keep it a secret. They'll find out soon enough.

For the same reason, except in rare instances don't repeat a trick. Sometimes a trick requires a repetition for greatest impact. But this doesn't happen very often.

Don't let the spectators annoy you, and certainly don't argue with them. An obnoxious member of the group says, "I know how you did that." There's no point in replying, "No, you don't, moron." Instead, say, "Sure, you do," and continue.

Other appropriate responses:

"Naturally."

"Absolutely."

"You bet."

If the ninny persists, say, "Glad to hear it. Now let's try this one."

Go ahead with the next trick.

Above all, enjoy yourself! Have you ever watched a magician on TV whose expression led you to believe he was suffering from severe indigestion? If performing magic bothers him so much, why is he doing it?

I've seen magicians at all levels of ability who are concentrating so intensely they seem to be in pain. If you're a person who can't enjoy performing magic, I highly recommend that you take up another hobby—one you can have fun with.

Magic not only *can* be fun, it *should* be fun.

—— Size of Coins ——

Readers from countries other than the United States may find it useful to know the size of the coins referred to in this book.

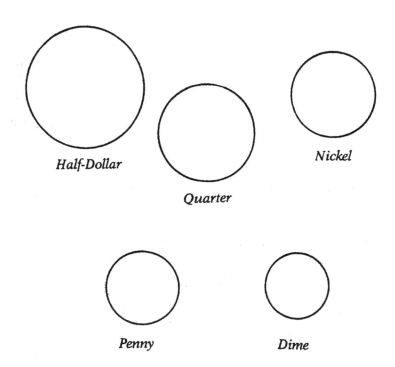

Half-Dollar

Quarter

Nickel

Penny

Dime

Coin Moves

The first seven items in this section explain how to make a coin disappear. Oddly enough, when magicians write about their methods of vanishing coins, they seldom include ways to make the coins reappear. Presumably a coin is placed into one hand, which is then shown empty, and the coin is revealed in the other hand. This is not magic, but absolute nonsense. Your audience is not made up of morons; they will eventually figure out that if the coin is not in one hand, it must be in the other. Therefore, the magician had better have clever ways to make the vanished coin reappear.

At the end of each of these seven items, I will provide a method for the coin to return. Obviously, you can mix and match the endings and the sleights.

The rest of this section consists of utility sleights that can be used in a variety of ways. For each item, I present a possible conclusion, raising the item from a slick maneuver to a befuddling trick.

The Palm

Some of the tricks in this book require you to palm a coin.

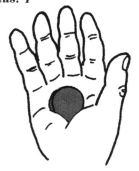

Illus. 1

Don't let the idea frighten you; it's really quite easy. Take a fifty-cent piece and place it in the palm of your right hand. Now cup your fingers slightly (Illus. 1). Turn the hand palm-down. Notice that the coin stays securely in place. Drop the hand to your side, still slightly cupped. The hand looks completely natural.

See? I told you it was easy. Here's a quick trick using the

basic palm. Place the fifty-cent piece on the palm of your hand, so that you can readily palm it. Open both hands, displaying the coin in your right hand and showing the empty left hand.

Bring the palm-up right hand over so that it is slightly forward of and below the palm-up left hand. As you do, cup the right hand so that the coin is now palmed. The left side of the right hand should be touching the ends of the fingers of the left hand (Illus. 2).

Illus. 2

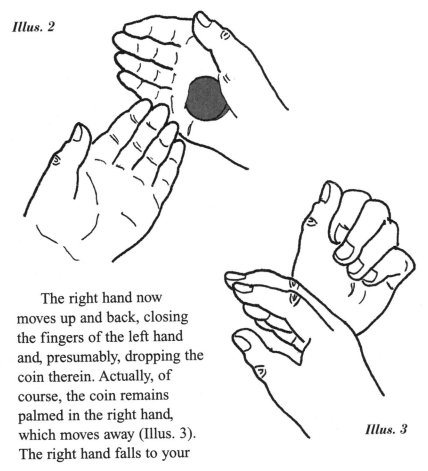

The right hand now moves up and back, closing the fingers of the left hand and, presumably, dropping the coin therein. Actually, of course, the coin remains palmed in the right hand, which moves away (Illus. 3). The right hand falls to your

Illus. 3

right side, while the closed left hand is held up for all to see.

To conclude, bend forward, placing your right hand behind your upper right leg. Slam the left hand down on the front of the leg, opening the hand as it reaches the leg. Lift the left hand away, showing it empty. Open the right hand and bring it forward, palm up, showing that the coin has evidently passed right through your leg.

The Thumb Palm

There are several variations of this sleight; this is the one that I prefer.

Hold the coin clipped between the first and second fingers of your right hand; the other fingers are folded back (Illus. 4).

Hold your left hand out, palm up. Place the coin on the palm of the left hand, retaining a grip on it with the first and second fingers of the right hand (Illus. 5). You will now move both hands simultane-

Illus. 4

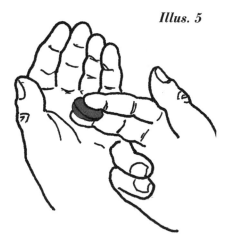

Illus. 5

ously. The left hand will turn clockwise; the right will turn counterclockwise. The first two fingers of the right hand bend inward, moving the coin into the fork formed by the thumb and first finger. The coin is clipped there by moving the thumb toward the first finger. *Instantly* extend the first two fingers again (Illus. 6).

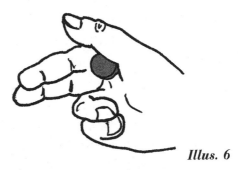

Illus. 6

The entire move is concealed by the left hand, which turns over

Illus. 7

clockwise and rests briefly on the back of the first two fingers of the right hand. The left hand next slides to the left and lightly grips the first two fingers of the right hand (Illus. 7). The left hand continues its sliding movement to the left, apparently removing the coin from the fingers. At the end of the movement, the left hand is in a fist, apparently holding the coin.

Your right hand drops to your side. As it does, raise the thumb slightly so that the coin drops onto your fingers. Bend forward slightly and bring your knees together. (Or, as in my case, bring them as close together as you can.)

Slap the left hand against the side of your left knee,

opening the hand as it makes contact. Then slap the right side of your right knee with the cupped right hand. Turn both hands palm-up. The left is empty; the right contains the coin. You must have magically passed it right through your legs.

The Slap Vanish

You'd think that an elementary vanish like this wouldn't fool many people. But what it lacks in subtlety, it more than makes up for in naturalness.

Hold a fifty-cent piece up in your right hand, gripping it between the first three fingers on one side and the thumb on the other (Illus. 8).

Bring it over to the palm-up, slightly cupped left hand.

Illus. 8

Slap it into the middle of the palm. Immediately close the left fingers and draw the right hand back.

Turn to Willie. "What do you think—heads or tails?"

He responds. Open the left hand, showing the coin. Comment on whether a head or tail is showing. "Let's try again."

With your right hand, move the coin to the tips of the left fingers, where it is gripped precisely as it was shown earlier with the right hand. Slap the coin into the right hand exactly as you slapped it into the left hand.

Again, ask Willie, "What do you think—heads or tails?" He responds.

Open the hand and show the coin. Comment on whether Willie was right.

"One more time."

Display the coin. Bring the right hand to the left. This time push the edge of the coin against the palm of the left hand, so that the fifty-cent piece is driven behind the right fingers. Move the right hand back as you close the left fingers. Let the right hand, slightly cupped, drop to your side. The coin rests on the ends of the right fingers.

Say to Willie, "Heads or tails?"

He makes his choice.

Slap your hands against your sides, a little above your middle. As your hands are about to land, open them up so that there's a simultaneous slap. Pause briefly. Lift away the left hand and show that it's empty.

"No, that isn't it. Let's try this one."

Take your right hand away from your body by first tilting it clockwise against your body, causing the coin to drop into your hand. Then take your hand away from your body and show the coin lying in your palm. Note whether it shows heads or tails and make an appropriate comment, based on Willie's choice.

One-Two-Three Trick

J. B. Bobo, master coin manipulator, came up with this original vanish. When I worked with it, I discovered a few weaknesses; the main weakness was that I had difficulty performing it. So I worked out this rather easier method.

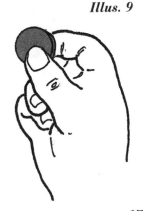

Illus. 9

Stand with your right side toward the spectators. In your right hand, hold a fifty-cent piece between the thumb on one side and the first and second fingers on the other (Illus. 9).

17

Illus. 10

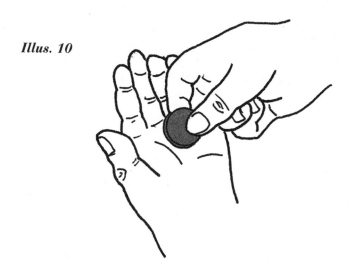

Place the coin into the palm of the left hand (Illus. 10). Close your left fingers over the coin *lightly*.

Retain your right-hand grip on the coin as you simultaneously turn the left hand clockwise and the right hand counterclockwise. Extend the right first finger, pointing at the left hand (Illus. 11). The coin is now gripped between the thumb and the right second and third fingers. You almost automatically grip the coin in this way.

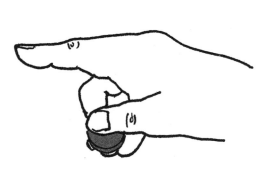

Illus. 11

Make an upward movement of the left hand, ostensibly tossing the coin upward. Turn to the front so that you're facing the group. As you do this, turn the right hand so that its

back is toward the group. Reach
up and out with your right
hand. Push the coin up with
your right thumb, so that it
appears suddenly at the tip of
your fingers (Illus. 12).

Why do I call this the One-
Two-Three Trick? Because it's a
three-count disappearance.

Count One: Place the coin
into the palm of the left hand.

Illus. 12

Count Two: Close the left fingers over the coin.

Count Three: Turn the hands, retaining the coin in the
right hand.

Drop It!

A variation of this splendid move is in my book *The Little
Giant Encyclopedia of Magic*. Here, the approach is different, and the conclusion is spectacular.

Your best bet is to reserve this move for when you're
seated at a table. Take out a large coin, preferably a fifty-cent
piece, and drop it onto the table. Pick it up with your left
hand, displaying it at your fingertips (Illus. 13). (Note that
the position is similar to that
shown in Illus. 12, but, in this
instance, the coin is held in
the *left* hand and it is also
held somewhat lower.) Shake
the hand a few times to
emphasize the importance of
the coin, and also to make it
logical that you would hold
the coin in such an unusual
position. At the same time,

Illus. 13

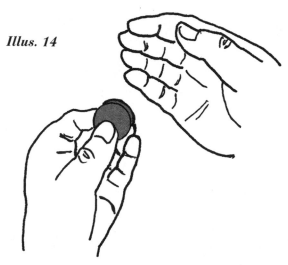

Illus. 14

you add emphasis by saying, "*This* ordinary-looking coin is quite magical. It has the power to pass through solid objects."

At this point you perform the sleight. Apparently, your right hand takes the coin from the left hand. Actually, the right hand approaches the left from above (Illus. 14). It appears that you grasp the coin between fingers and thumb; actually, you simply move your *left thumb* back slightly, releasing the coin and allowing it to drop down to the base of the left fingers. At the

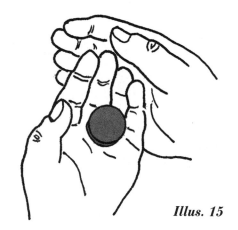

Illus. 15

same time, seemingly grasp the coin with your right hand (Illus. 15).

Hold the right hand up, evidently displaying the coin (Illus. 16). At the same time, say, "For example!" The left hand, slightly cupped, has dropped to the table. (No need to worry about palming the coin, it will stay secure in the cupped hand.)

Illus. 16

Slam the right hand onto the table, palm down. Simultaneously, stick your left hand under the table. Turn your right hand over, showing that the coin is gone.

Bring your left hand out palm-up, demonstrating that the coin has passed through the table.

Note

If spectators are seated on all sides, you might want to push your seat back from the table before performing the sleight. Then move back in to perform the latter part of the trick.

A Hot Revolver

How about a simple, effective vanish? Your right side is toward the audience. Hold a large coin in the right hand between the thumb and the fingertips of the first three fingers.

Display the coin. You will now appear to put the coin into the left hand and close the left fingers over it. Start by putting the edge of the coin into the cupped left hand (Illus. 17). Note that it is placed just below the base of the fingers.

You now perform two actions simultaneously. You close the fingers of the left hand, ostensibly over the coin. At the same time, you move the left hand to the right, causing the coin to revolve counterclockwise. The coin moves under the

21

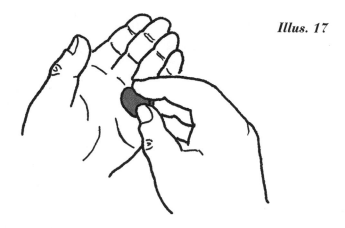

right fingers, where it is held concealed between fingers and thumb. *Throughout this move, the right hand does not move at all.* The coin is revolved by the action of the left hand only.

Finally, raise the closed left hand and casually drop your right hand to your side. The coin drops naturally to the fingers of the cupped hand.

Hold up your left hand. Slip your right hand into the right forward pocket of your slacks. The hand goes into the pocket with your palm toward the body, so that spectators will not observe the coin. Immediately turn the hand over and open the fingers.

Bring the left fist rapidly toward your leg on the outside of the pocket. Just before slapping it down, open the fingers. The left hand should be hitting precisely on the spot where you have the coin in your pocket.

Lift up your left hand, showing that it is empty. Remove the right hand from your pocket, palm up. Let everyone see that the coin has evidently passed right through the cloth and into your right hand.

Another Vanish

To all appearances, you drop a coin from your right hand to your left. Of course that's only an illusion.

This clever move was developed by Tom Sullivan. My version, including the ending, is slightly different. Although the move itself is quite simple, you will need considerable practice to make it seem completely natural.

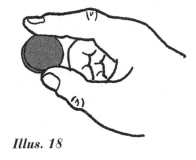

Hold a coin at opposite edges between the right first finger and thumb. Display it at eye level (Illus. 18). Announce whether the audience is looking at a head or a tail. For instance,

Illus. 18

if you're looking at a tail, the group must be seeing a head, so you say, "Notice that on this side you see a head."

Drop your right hand to belt level, revolving your hand so the group can see the other side of the coin (Illus. 19). "And on this side you see a tail."

Bring your *left* hand up so that it's a few inches to the left

Illus. 19

of the right hand. Your left hand should be palm-up and slightly cupped. Bring the right hand to the left so that the right little finger lands just inside the left fingertips (Illus. 20). Revolve the right hand back toward you so that the fingers are pointed downward. Release your grip on the coin. Apparently you're dumping the coin into the left hand. Actually, it comes to rest on the ends of the right fingers. The

Illus. 20

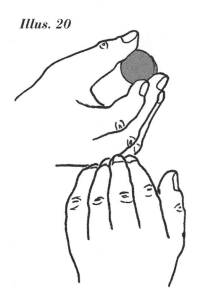

sneakiness is concealed by the left fingers.

Naturally, you close your left fingers as the coin drops. This creates the illusion that the coin has dropped into the left hand.

The right hand, holding the coin, is now slightly cupped. *Don't move it.* Instead, move the left hand up and to the left. Let your eyes follow the movement of the left hand. Still gazing at the left hand, address Janet: "What do you suppose the coin will be—heads or tails?"

Close the right hand and turn it palm-down. Smack your left hand onto its back, as though positioning the coin there.

If necessary, repeat the question: "What'll it be—heads or tails?"

If she does not reply, or if someone starts to express legitimate doubt as to the whereabouts of the coin, say, "Let's take a look and see what we have."

Don't worry about interrupting; this is no time to be concerned about the fine points of politeness.

Rub your left hand against the back of the right hand. Lift up the left hand, showing that your hand is empty and the coin is gone. "Uh-oh! We have nothing. I think I slapped it down too hard."

Turn your right hand over and open it. Suppose a head is showing. "It's heads, Janet," you say. Depending on what was called, either congratulate Janet or express regret that she missed.

Note

As you practice this sleight, frequently try it out in front of a mirror. Legitimately drop the coin, and then do the sleight. As much as possible, try to duplicate the natural movement of dropping the coin into the left hand.

As I've already mentioned, in every sleight you should check the legitimate move and then try to match it with the trick move. Give each move plenty of practice, and don't attempt any trick until you can make the basic sleight seem completely natural.

An Extra Revelation

Presumably you've placed the coin into your left hand, but actually it's palmed in your right. We'll assume that you've performed "The Palm," described on pages 12 and 13.

With the right first finger, point to the left hand. Slowly open the left hand one finger at a time, starting with the little finger. Much to everyone's astonishment, the coin is gone.

Lift your hands to head level. Open them so that they are palm-up. The hands should be tilted back slightly (Illus. 21). No one will be able to see the coin in your right hand.

Illus. 21

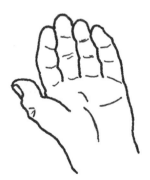
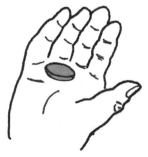

Lower your left hand. Bring the right hand down and slap it onto the open left hand, leaving the coin there. *Do not close either hand.* Immediately repeat the action twice, as though applauding. Lift the right hand and move it aside, showing that the coin has reappeared in the left hand.

Note

If you do it properly, no one will see the coin when you do the slapping motion. The key is to keep the receiving hand slightly cupped and tilted back toward yourself.

The Finger Palm

This is a paradoxical move. It's not strong enough to be the only basic move in a trick, but it's one of the most useful of all the tricky moves. As you might gather, it's actually not a sleight at all. In fact, it's simply a way to keep a coin, or some other small object, concealed.

Illus. 22

Take a fifty-cent piece into your right hand. Grip it in your third and fourth fingers (Illus. 22). The coin is secured on one side just beyond the first joint of the fingers and on the other by the palm. Let your hand drop to your side, slightly cupped. That's it! The coin is satisfactorily hidden.

Other common ways to hold the coin in the finger palm is with the first and second fingers or the second and third fingers.

Easy, huh? No wonder I don't think of it as a sleight.

The Switch 1

In each of the next two sleights, you're going to switch one coin for another. In this first one, you'll magically change a quarter into a fifty-cent piece. In doing so, you'll be using several of the moves described above.

Now for the trick. Before performing, place a fifty-cent piece and a quarter into your right front pocket. Ready? First, reach into the pocket and place the half-dollar into position for "The Finger Palm" (page 26). Then clip the quarter between the first two fingers in the position for "The Thumb Palm" (page 14). Bring your hand out, displaying the quarter (Illus. 23).

Take the coin into your left hand. Hold it up, displaying it. "For those of you who are sitting at the back, here we have a quarter," you announce.

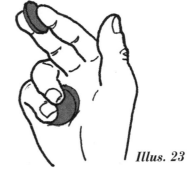

Illus. 23

Return the coin to its original position in the right hand. Hold it up again, saying, "Yes, worth a full twenty-five cents." Nobody will see the fifty-cent piece so long as you keep the back of the hand toward the group.

With your right hand, you're now going to close the left hand with a motion similar to that used for "The Palm" (page 12). If you look at the illustrations accompanying that sleight, you'll get the drift of the move to use.

As your right hand starts to close the left, you thumb-palm the quarter and, simultaneously, drop the fifty-cent piece into the left hand. ("The Thumb Palm" is described on page 14.) Actually, in doing the thumb palm, you almost automatically drop the fifty-cent piece. Don't worry about performing a speedy thumb palm. Just perform it as smoothly as you can; no one will catch the move. When the hand is completely closed, the right hand continues moving back a bit. Then it drops to your side.

Hold up the closed left hand. At the same time, let the quarter drop onto your right fingers. Look at your left hand, saying, "But can you make money with a mere quarter? The answer is, yes."

Open the hand and let all see that the quarter has changed into a fifty-cent piece. At the same time, with the right hand, push the quarter back and hold it in the finger palm, on the third and fourth fingers. (See "The Finger Palm," page 26.)

"In fact, it can *double* in value."

Bring the right hand to the coin and grasp it between the first two fingers and the thumb. Hold it up.

Stick your right hand into your pocket. Let loose of the quarter, but retain your grip on the fifty-cent piece. Bring it out, saying, "Oh, incidentally, it *is* a real half-dollar." Hand it to a spectator. "Examine it if you wish."

The Switch 2

You may prefer to use this switch, which is somewhat easier than the one described above.

Again, you start with a fifty-cent piece and a quarter in your right front pocket. Reach in and, as before, get the fifty-cent piece in a finger palm—that is, grip it with the third and fourth fingers. (See "The Finger Palm," page 26.)

The quarter is gripped between the first and second fingers on one side and your thumb on the other.

Take your right hand from the pocket and display the quarter. Toss the quarter into the left hand, closing the hand as soon as the coin arrives. Pick it up and, presumably, toss it in again. Actually, you slide the quarter back a bit with your right thumb and toss the fifty-cent piece instead. Once more, make sure that you close the left hand immediately.

To drop the fifty-cent piece, all you need do is release pressure on the third and fourth fingers of the right hand. Barely any movement is involved.

To perfect the move, be sure to try it the regular way and then the trick way, trying to match the moves exactly. Be sure to check it out in a mirror.

If you decide to try this switch, I suggest you follow the patter and routine described in "Switch 1."

—— Coin Tricks ——

A Falling Off

For this trick, you'll need four coins—quarters or fifty-cent pieces. Whichever you choose, all four should look alike. In other words, you shouldn't have two old dingy coins and two new shiny ones; if you do, the secret of the trick may be revealed.

Let's assume that you're using quarters. Toss them out onto the table. Pick up one in each hand. Close your hands into fists and turn them over so that the nails are up. The coins should be completely concealed (Illus. 24).

Indicate that you need an assistant. Choose Marilyn from the many eager volunteers who are shrieking, "Pick me, pick me!"

Illus. 24

Say to her, "Marilyn, please put one quarter on each of my hands—right on the fingernails."

She does (Illus. 25).

"When I turn my hands over, the coins fall off, of course."

At the word "over," turn the hands over, so that a few inches separate them.

Illus. 25

The assumption is that the coins placed on your fingernails fall to the table. In reality, you drop both coins from the left hand. The coin on the left fingernails drops easily, of course, and you drop the other coin by opening the fingers only slightly and quickly closing them again. The right hand actually performs a similar move, with this difference: The fingers open slightly as you execute the circular inward move, only you *grab* the coin that's on the fingernails rather than release it.

Turn the hands back, fingernails up once more. Say to Marilyn, "Let's do it differently this time. Please put both coins on either hand. Just pick a hand and put *both* coins on the fingernails."

She does.

"Watch carefully."

Separate the hands widely. Make a snappy upward movement with both hands, opening them up so that they are slightly cupped. The coins resting on the fingernails drop into the hand. You now either have four coins in the right hand and none in the left, or two coins in each hand. Drop both hands and hold them out, displaying the coins.

Either way, you have a miracle. Depending on the situation, say, "And now we have four coins in one hand, and none in the other." Or say, "Once more, we have two coins in each hand."

Cross-Up

The preceding trick, this one, and the next one comprise an excellent routine. This trick, which originally appeared in my *World's Best Coin Tricks*, fits in so perfectly that I thought it was worth a repeat.

You'll need either two half-dollars or two quarters.

(1) Start with your hands crossed at the wrists, palms up. One coin is in each palm (Illus. 26).

(2) Form the hands into loose fists and turn them over, keeping the wrists crossed (Illus. 27). As you form the fists,

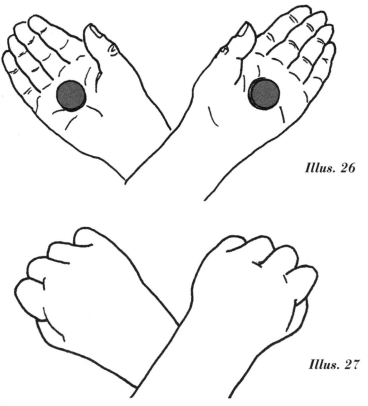

Illus. 26

Illus. 27

palm the coin that's in the right hand. (See "The Palm," page 12.)

(3) Move both hands to the left, opening the left hand and dropping its coin to the table.

(4) Still keeping the wrists crossed, pick up the coin with the left fingers and thumb. Form a loose fist, holding the coin on the fingertips.

(5) Move the hands to the right. Simultaneously drop the coin from the left fingers *(without opening the hand)* and open the right hand, but retain the coin in the palm.

(6) Hands still crossed, pick up the coin on the table with the right fingers and thumb.

(7) Slowly and deliberately separate your hands. Smack both fists on the table. Turn the hands over and open them, showing that the coins are now in the same hand.

An alternative ending: Put your right hand under the table. Smack the left palm on the table. Shake the coins in the right hand so that there is at least one pronounced clink. Turn over the left hand and lift it, showing that the coin is gone. Bring out the right hand, showing the two coins.

Get Your Teeth into It

Many decades ago, I saw this trick presented by renowned magician J. B. Bobo. I loved the trick and his clever handling. *But*...he kept putting a coin between his teeth. I'm not a squeamish person. For instance, I can't think of an action a baseball player would perform that would make me ill. Still, I hate the idea of putting anything as filthy as a coin into my mouth. So I worked out a slick device that retains the subtlety of Bobo's routine, keeps the diseased coin from contacting my teeth, and actually adds a humorous touch.

You'll need two fifty-cent pieces and a paper napkin or a tissue. In a pinch, you could use your handkerchief.

Toss two fifty-cent pieces onto the table.

"I'm now going to attempt something magical with these coins. As I do so, I'll explain every single step so that everyone will understand precisely what I'm doing and why. Unfortunately, the magician who taught me this actually put the coins into his mouth. I find that idea *extremely* unhygienic, so I'll use this."

Show the napkin.

"Please listen carefully so that you'll understand the trick perfectly."

Stuff the middle of the napkin into your mouth. The bulk of the napkin remains outside. From this point on, you say nothing that is in the least distinguishable. You keep making nonsense sounds with more and less emphasis as though explaining what's going on.

Pick up the coin on the left and place it between your teeth, which are now protected by the napkin. Pick up the coin on the right and show it, bouncing it on your palm until you have it in the regular palming position. If you'll read "The Palm," beginning on page 12, an excellent vanish is explained at the end. You now go through the motions of this vanish, but actually place the coin into your left hand.

With your right hand, take the coin from your mouth; with your left, place the other coin between your teeth.

Again, show the coin in your right hand and place it into the left hand.

Again, with your right hand, take the coin from your mouth; with your left, place the other coin between your teeth.

To simplify, you actually pass the coin from your right hand to your left two times. The third time, however...

Show the coin in your right hand, bouncing it into palming position. Perform the sleight, retaining the coin in the palm of your right hand.

The situation: You have a coin between your teeth and one in your right hand. The left hand, in a palm-up fist, stays put.

Take the coin from your mouth with the right hand, which now contains two coins—one in your palm and one held between fingers and thumb. Take this right hand behind your right knee. Bring the left hand down and slap it against the knee, opening the hand just before it hits. Shake the right hand so that the coins rattle. Turn the left hand over, showing that the coin is gone. Bring out the right hand and show that two coins are there; one has apparently passed through your knee.

Provide one last incoherent explanation with the napkin in your mouth. Then remove the napkin and proceed to your next trick.

The Great Escape

How about a unique trick, one that you can do again and again, while observers have virtually no idea of what you're up to? What's more, the trick requires no particular skill, other than the ability to chat extemporaneously.

As I explain, everything will be much clearer to you if you follow along with actual coins.

The trick is based on this principle: Suppose you were to take six coins and place them into a row, like this:

     1   3   2

From left to right, you have one coin, then a pile of three coins, and finally a pile of two coins. Below (nearer to you) the single coin, you place a pile of three coins:

     1   3   2
     3

Below the pile of two coins, you place another pile of three coins:

     1   3   2
     3   3

Finally, you take six coins and place them into a row below the other coins (two coins, then three, and finally one):

1	3	2
3		3
2	3	1

The coins form a square. Naturally, every square has four sides. In this instance, each of the four sides adds up to 6. Let's say that you point this out to a friend. (You *never* point out to him the actual total of coins, which in this instance is 18.) Then say, "Please remove one coin." He does so, leaving this:

1	2	2
3		3
2	3	1

Can you rearrange the remaining coins so that each side will still total 6? Of course you can. Here is one possible way. Take a coin from the pile of 3 on the right side and place it on the pile of 2 just above it:

1	2	3
3		2
2	3	1

The actual total of coins is 17, but you don't point this out. Instead, you count each of the sides, showing that each side still totals 6.

Your friend removes another coin, leaving this:

1	2	3
3		2
2	2	1

Can you rearrange the coins to make each side total 6? Sure. Just take a coin from the pile of 3 on the left side. Place this coin on the pile of 2 just below it:

1	2	3
2		2
3	2	1

You'd now point out that each side still adds up to 6. How many more times can you do this? You can do it twice more, ending up with 14 coins and this configuration:

2	1	3
1		1
3	1	2

The key is this: The fewer coins you have, the more coins you have in the corners. When you have 18 coins, the coins in the corners total 6. When you have 17 coins, those in the corners total 7. When you have 16 coins, the coins in the corners total 8. And when you have 14 coins, those in the corners total 10. Therefore, *every time a spectator takes a coin, you add a coin to one of the corners.*

Now comes the bad news: The above is not the trick. If you use this modest number of coins, some spectators might catch on. Instead, I'll explain how you can use 34 coins. *Eight* times you'll take a coin away, yet the number apparently remains the same. I'll explain in considerable detail how you accomplish this. The purpose is to give you a better idea of the basic principle. But you actually should never do the stunt eight separate times. At the end, I explain how you can present an amusing trick in which you first take one coin away and make it reappear, and do the rest of the coins in groups.

But first, removing one coin at a time. All you need do each time is add a coin to one of the corners and rearrange the remaining coins so that each row and column has a pile of 1, 2, 3, and 4.

(As before, everything will be much clearer if you will follow along using actual coins. I generally use pennies.)

Let's run through the basic trick. Later, I'll tell you how to make it truly entertaining.

You'll need 34 pennies. You're going to build a square, starting with the corners. You'll want the smallest number of pennies possible in each corner:

1	2
2	1

If you want the smallest number possible, why don't you put a single coin in each corner? Because each side must have a pile of 4 coins, a pile of 3 coins, a pile of 2 coins, and a single coin. If each corner had a single coin in it, this would be impossible.

Currently every side has a single coin and a pile of 2 coins. You can add the piles of 3 and 4 coins anywhere you wish, so long as each side has one of each type. Here's a possibility:

1	4	3	2
3			4
4			3
2	3	4	1

Note that each side of the square has four piles of coins—one pile of four coins, one pile of three coins, one pile of two coins, and a single coin. (From now on, I'll refer to this as a set of *1234*, regardless of its order.) The *order* of these piles will vary. Naturally, each side will total 10 coins—the total of 4, 3, 2, and 1.

The rules (for you):

(1) Each side must have four piles.

(2) Each side must have a number of coins that total 10.

(3) Each side must have a set of *1234*.

(4) If a spectator removes a coin from a corner, you replace the coin before proceeding.

(5) Every time a spectator takes a coin, you add a coin to one of the corners.

Here is how the trick proceeds:

You count each side for the spectators. You start by moving along the near side, moving from left to right, touching each pile as you count it. "Here we have 2...and 3 is 5...and 4 is 9...and 1 is 10."

You would then move from left to right along the top side. "Here's 1...and 4 is 5...and 3 is 8...and 2 is 10."

You do the same sort of count coming *down* the left side. Finally, you count to 10, coming *down* the right side.

You follow this exact procedure every time you count the coins.

Let's proceed with the trick. Say to a spectator, "Please pick up one coin from one of the sides and hand it to me."

You place the coin into your pocket. Show that your hands are absolutely empty, and then redistribute the remaining coins so that each side has a number of coins that total 10, formed by a set of *1234*.

This is quite easy, as you'll see. All you need do is *keep track of the corner coins*. At the beginning, you have the minimum number of coins in the corners. And you've filled in with piles of 3 and 4. The spectator has removed a coin. Let's say that he has taken one from the pile of 3 in the bottom row:

1	4	3	2
3			4
4			3
2	2	4	1

Your first step is to take any coin from one of the sides and add it to a corner. Which corner? Obviously, you cannot add a coin to the upper left corner, for that would give you two piles of 2 on the left side and along the upper side; this would prevent either side from having a set of *1234*. For the same reason, you can't add a coin to the lower right corner. So you must add a coin to one of the corner piles of 2. Let's add a coin to the lower left corner. The formation now looks like this:

1	4	3	2
3			4
4			3
3	2	4	1

Once you've adjusted the corners, you neither take nor add to the corners until after the spectator has removed another coin.

So it's time to fill in the sides. Following the same order as you do when you count the coins, you start on the bottom row. In the bottom corners you have a pile of 3 coins and a 1-coin pile. That interior pile of 3 needs to become a pile of 2, so you pick up a coin from that pile. The entire layout at this point:

1	4	3	2
2			3
4			3
3	2	4	1

You now move to the top side. Everything works. You have a *1234* set.

Look down the left side. That side also has a *1234* set. This must be your lucky day.

Now the right side. At the ends we have a pile of 2 and a pile of 1 (which makes a very small pile). And we have two

piles of 3 in the middle. What a stroke of luck! You're holding a coin. Add it to one of the piles of 3.

The present layout:

1	4	3	2
2			4
4			3
3	2	4	1

We proceed to count the coins again. As before, we count
from left to right along the bottom, getting 10. Next we count
from left to right along the top. Then we count down the left
side. Finally, we count down the right side. And each side
totals 10. The coin must be back!

Again the spectator takes a coin and hands it over. You
slip it into your pocket, and then readjust the remaining
coins.

As always, the only real concern is the corners. You must
add a coin from the sides to one of the corners. Once more, if
you add a coin to a 1-coin pile, you'll have an extra pile of 2
in one of the rows. So we'd better form another pile of 3:

1	2	3	3
2			4
4			3
3	2	4	1

You fill in to make each side a perfect *1234*, and then
count the sides for the spectator.

In all, the spectator takes 8 coins. Each time he takes a
coin, you add one coin to a corner and fill in to form a *1234*
on each side. Here's the recommended corner position each
time:

(A) 1	2	(B) 1	2	(C) 1	3
2	1	3	1	3	1

(D) 2	3	(E) 2	3	(F) 2	3
3	1	3	2	4	2

(G) 2	4	(H) 3	4	(I) 3	4
4	2	4	2	4	3

As you study the various positions, an obvious pattern emerges. In B, you'll note that you add a coin to one of the higher-numbered corners; in C, you add a coin to the other higher-numbered corner, evening up these two corners.

In D, you add a coin to one of the lower-numbered corners; in E, you add a coin to the other lower-numbered corner, evening up these two corners.

The next four items follow this pattern exactly. In F as in B, a coin is added to one of the higher-numbered corners. In G, an added coin evens up the higher-numbered corners. In H, you add a coin to one of the lower-numbered corners. And in I, equality is sought as a coin is added to the other lower-numbered corner.

The key to the trick is to tend to the corners. It's quite easy to fill in once you have the proper number of coins in each corner. Your starting position is A. A spectator hands you one of the coins, which you place in your pocket. You *know* that you must go to position B. This means you must take a coin from somewhere other than a corner and add it to a pile of two in one of the corners, thus ending up with:

(B) 1	3
2	1

Then all you need do is fill in so that every row is a *1234* combination. The specifics of your later moves are not important. You might move as many as five coins before you end up with four sets of *1234*. Or you might move only one coin. *Many other* arrangements are possible. The procedure I recommend is the one that I find easiest and most logical.

Following the moves above, you can perform this wonderful reappearance eight times. A mighty slick trick!

As clever as this trick is, I'm not sure how interesting it would be without some sort of plot. One that I developed is a tale of World War II Allied prisoners, based on an old television show.

Also, the moves are much easier than those I describe above. The previous explanation was an attempt to make clear the *basic principle* behind the moves. The method given for this version of the trick is quite simple, as you'll see.

Start by laying out the 34 coins where all four sides contain a *1234* form. This, for instance, is the one I recommended earlier:

```
1    4    3    2
3              4
4              3
2    3    4    1
```

As you lay out the coins, explain:

"During World War II, a number of Allied prisoners were being held in Stalag 71...or, as it was called in German, 'Shtahlahg sefenty-vun.' In charge of the camp was one Colonel Klunk, who was actually stupid enough to be two Colonel Klunks. Now here's the camp."

With your first finger, draw a large square around the square of coins.

"And every day, Colonel Klunk would have the prisoners line up in a square..."

Indicate the square of coins.

"...and he'd count them...*personally*." Pause. "I told you he wasn't too bright. Now here's the way he'd count them."

As described above, you count the coins along the bottom or near side; the total, of course, is 10. You then count, in order, the coins along the top side, the right side, and the left side. In each instance, the total is 10.

If you can count in a horrible German accent, wonderful; if not, don't worry about it.

"Notice that each side totaled 10. One night, a prisoner escaped." Address Annie: "Would you sneak a prisoner out from anywhere." She takes a coin. Hold out your hand so that she hands you the coin. You put the coin into your pocket, saying, "He disappeared into the darkness."

"Later that night, Corporal Schlitz, who was almost as bright as Colonel Klunk, came to Klunk and told him, 'I tink vun uf der prisoners is missink.' So Colonel Klunk ordered everyone out of the barracks." Show that your hands are completely empty. "All the Allied prisoners came out, moved around, and lined up."

Set up the corner coins in the B formation. An easier way to put it is: Add one coin to the lower left corner.

(B) 1   2
    3   1

Fill in the remaining spaces, completing *1234* sets.

Have Colonel Klunk count the soldiers. When the count is finished, continue, "So Colonel Klunk turned on Schlitz, saying, '*Dumkopf!* All se prisoners are here.' And he returned to his quarters."

Each time prisoners escape, they "disappear into the darkness," as you place the chosen coins into your pocket.

"A little later, Corporal Schlitz woke up Colonel Klunk, who was very angry, 'Vy did you vake me up? I suppose you tink anuzzer prisoner has escaped.' 'No, *mein mir bis du schoen*. I tink *two* prisoners haf escaped.'"

Address Annie: "Would you liberate two prisoners, please?" Take the two from Annie and put them into your pocket, saying, "And they, too, disappeared into the darkness."

To correct for the missing prisoners, you must skip C and move to D. Actually, all you need do is add one coin to each of the *top two corners*.

(D) 2   3
     3   1

Move *two* coins to the appropriate corners and adjust the other coins accordingly.

Have Colonel Klunk count the prisoners and then hurl abuse at Schlitz. "Vot's the meaning of zis, Schlitz?"

"Vell, Colonel [cough]..."

"That's a dumb cough, *dumkopf.* Don't bother me again."

The following night, two more prisoners escape. Again, Klunk should abuse Schlitz.

You arrange the corner coins as in F. To put it another way, simply add one coin to each of the *bottom two corners*.

     2   3
     4   2

You fill in as before. Once again, the count seems to be correct.

"The following night, *three* Allied prisoners escaped." Annie is asked to remove three coins from the sides and hand them to you. As you put them into your pocket, you repeat, "And, of course, they disappeared into the darkness. Naturally, Schlitz noticed what was going on, and—ever loyal—he woke up his leader. 'Colonel, Colonel, vake up!'

"'Vat now, Schlitz—two more prisoners haf escaped?'

"'*Nein, mein schwein. Three* more prisoners haf escaped.'

"The Colonel cursed savagely: 'Oh, *du schoener schnitzelbank!'*

"Then he ordered the prisoners out for another lineup."

This is the last time you'll rearrange the coins. This time, it's particularly easy. Two corners must have four coins, and two must have three coins. The two piles of four must be diagonal from each other, and the same for the two piles of three. In other words, you use the I formation:

(I) 3   4

    4   3

As always, you fill in, completing the necessary *1234*s.

For the final time, Colonel Klunk counts the prisoners. "'Vell, Schlitz, everybody iss still here. Vot do you make uf dat?'

"'I'll tell you later.'

"Later that night, Schlitz gathered up all the rest of the prisoners..." Pick up all the rest of the coins. "...and took off, leaving a note that said, 'I qvit.'

"And so do I..." (put all the coins in your pocket) "...as they all disappear into the darkness."

Review

(1) Start with 34 coins.

(2) Place a coin in the upper left corner, two in the upper right corner, two in the lower left corner, and one in the lower right corner. Fill in to form four sets of *1234*. Count the sides, showing that each adds to 10.

(3) Here are the corner combinations for the patter version, after the original layout:

(A) One coin is removed. Add a coin to the lower left corner.

(B) Two coins are removed. Add a coin to each of the upper corners.

(C) Two coins are removed. Add a coin to each of the lower corners.

(D) Three coins are removed. Make sure you have piles of three in diagonal corners and piles of four in the other corners.

(4) Remember: If a spectator removes a coin from a corner, replace it before proceeding.

Notes

(1) Whenever the coins are laid out, they should overlap or, even better, be separate. This way, the correct number in each pile can be readily observed by onlookers. Also, this helps when you're rearranging the coins.

(2) If you can do a German accent, you can provide amusing exchanges between Schlitz and Klunk as the trick proceeds.

Which Way Did They Go?

As far as I can discover, "The Great Escape" is actually a variation of this original trick, which involved adding coins to the square rather than taking them away. As you will see, you begin with 26 coins forming a square. Eight coins are placed in the middle. One by one, they seem to disappear.

To further confuse you, this trick is the *exact opposite* of the previous stunt. If you understand the previous trick, you just start at the end and work your way to the beginning.

Let's give it a try. Set the coins out as follows:

3	2	1	4
1			2
2			1
4	1	2	3

This, of course, is the final layout of the previous trick.

Announce, "As another of my weird experiments, I'm going to attempt the impossible. I'm going to try to make coins disappear before your very eyes."

Put eight coins in the middle of the formation. As described in the previous trick, count the coins in each row. Each row comes to 10, of course. Pick up one coin from the middle pile. Place it anywhere except in one of the corners.

Then arrange the corners so that they match the second last formation, H:

```
        3    4
        4    2
```

Fill in so that groups of *1234* are on all sides. Count each side, *proving* that a coin has vanished.

"One gone. Let's try again." Pick out another coin from the middle and add it to one of the sides.

You then proceed as before. You can continue until you vanish eight coins, one at a time. Or you can quit somewhere along the way if you choose. For convenience, here is the order of the corner positions. It is identical to the one I showed in the previous trick, except that it is reversed. To avoid confusion, I'm using the same identifying letters as before. I'll start with the original position:

(I) 3	4	(H) 3	4	(G) 2	4
4	3	4	2	4	2

(F) 2	3	(E) 2	3	(D) 2	3
4	2	3	2	3	1

(C) 1	3	(B) 1	2	(A) 1	2
3	1	3	1	2	1

Note
It probably goes without saying that "The Great Escape" and "Which Way Did They Go?" should not be done in the same set.

Put a Spin on It
How about a nifty quick trick? You may use any size coin, but because there is a sense of touch involved, you should always use the same size.

Let's assume that you elect to use a quarter. Toss it into the palm of the right hand (Illus. 28). Move the hand upward, tossing the coin into the air. Much to everyone's astonishment, the coin *spins* precisely as it would had you flicked it

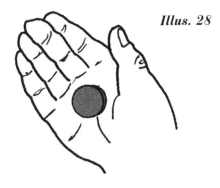

Illus. 28

into the air with your thumb.

Regardless of whether anyone has noticed the spinning, you say, "Did you notice the spinning of the coin?" The answer doesn't matter. "I'll show you again."

You perform the stunt again.

Let others try it. No way. You're the only one who can do it. How?

Simple. You perform the upward move. Stick your thumb out above the palm. The thumb flicks the edge of the coin, which is moving upward. This is what spins the coin. Because of the larger movement of the hand, the insertion of the thumb goes unnoticed.

Try the trick; it works.

Cups and Coins

You'll need two cups that you can't see through and seven pennies and seven dimes.

I saw this trick performed some time ago by a young lad who used red and black checkers. The only problem was that it was perfectly obvious what he was doing. This can be avoided by simply using smaller objects—in this instance, pennies and dimes.

I highly recommend that you try this trick out; it's actually fairly simple once you've mastered the basic moves, *and* it's a real reputation-maker.

To begin with, you should have all but one of the coins in your left pants pocket. One of the pennies should be in your right pants pocket.

Besides the objects, you'll also need two assistants. Betty and Julie seemed to like the show so far; why not ask them to help out?

Have Betty stand to your left and Julie stand to your right. Hold a cup in your right hand, straight out from your right shoulder. The cup should be extended in front of you. Say to Betty, "Please hold the cup just like this, Betty."

Hand her one of the cups.

Hold the other cup in your *left* hand, straight out from your left shoulder. Again, the cup should be extended in front of you. Say to Julie, "And would you please hold the cup just like this, Julie."

Hand Julie the other cup.

Reach both hands into your pockets. With your left hand, grab all of the coins from your left pocket, saying, "Oh, here they are." Meanwhile, with your right hand, take the penny from your right pants pocket, holding it in "The Finger Palm" (page 26).

Show the coins in your left hand. Say, "Here we have pennies and dimes. Betty, we'll try to give everyone an equal deal."

With the right hand, pick up a penny from your left palm, using the first two fingers and the thumb. Hold up the coin so that all can see it. Reach your hand out, dip it into Betty's cup slightly, and drop the penny.

Illus. 29

(Throughout the trick, you'll always pick up the coin between the first two fingers and thumb. Following this, you'll always hold up the coin so that all can see it [Illus. 29].

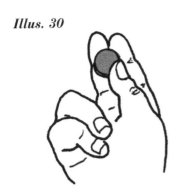

Illus. 30

After showing the coin, pull it down with your thumb so that it is concealed behind your first two fingers [Illus. 30]. Finally, you'll reach your hand out and dip it into the cup slightly. At this point, you'll either drop the coin you've just shown or you'll drop the coin you're holding in the finger palm.)

Address Betty, "To be fair, you should also get a dime."

Pick a dime from your left hand. Hold it up so that all can see it. Dip your right hand into Betty's cup slightly, letting the penny fall from your finger palm. (Since your hand is slightly inside the cup, the move is absolutely undetectable. Because you have moved the dime behind your first two fingers, no one can see it as you withdraw your hand. As you move the right hand away from the cup, draw the coin to the right with your thumb so that it drops into a loose version of the finger palm. You are now able to pick up a coin in the right hand, between the first two fingers and thumb.)

There are now two pennies in Betty's cup. Everyone believes that the cup contains a penny and a dime.

"Your turn, Julie. Let's start with a dime."

Pick a dime from your left hand, show it, and drop it into Julie's cup.

"To be fair, we'll have to also give you a penny."

Pick up a penny, show it, and pretend to drop it into Julie's cup. Actually, you drop the dime you're holding in the finger palm.

This entire routine will be repeated three times. Each time you start out with a penny finger-palmed in your right hand.

(1) You take a penny and put it into Betty's cup.

(2) You take a dime and pretend to put it into Betty's cup. Actually, you let the penny drop from your finger palm.

(3) You draw the dime aside with your thumb so that it falls into a loose finger palm.

You turn to Julie.

(4) You take a dime and put it into Julie's cup.

(5) You take a penny and pretend to put it into Julie's cup. Actually, you let the dime drop from your finger palm.

(6) You draw the penny aside with your thumb so that it falls into a loose finger palm.

Apparently you're dropping pennies and dimes into each cup. Actually, Betty's cup holds only pennies, and Julie's cup holds only dimes.

So you have performed the same routine three times. Betty has six pennies in her cup; Julie has six dimes in her cup. You are holding a penny finger-palmed in your right hand, and a dime is resting on the palm of your left hand.

There is no reason that anyone should know how many coins you originally held in your left hand. Nor, at the end, should anyone know how many coins you have left. To insure this, close your left hand slightly as you near the end.

Your final move is as follows: Reach into the right hand, taking the dime between the first two fingers and thumb. At the same time, drop the finger-palmed penny into the left hand. Turn both hands palm-up, showing the coins.

Drop the dime into Julie's cup, saying, "Here's an extra dime for you, Julie."

Drop the penny into Betty's cup, saying, "And here's an extra penny for you, Betty." Pause. "Please don't argue about it; I had to get rid of them *some* way."

Take the cup from Julie. "Let's see what you have, Julie."

Spill out the cup, showing that she has all dimes. "My goodness, but you're greedy."

Take Betty's cup and spill out the pennies. "Oh, poor Betty. She gets stuck with all the pennies."

Turn to the group. "How about a nice hand for my wonderful assistants, Betty and Julie!" Lead the applause yourself.

This, by the way, is one of the marvelously sneaky ways by which you can get applause. That's right, just ask for applause for whoever assists you. The group *likes* to applaud; they're just not sure *when*.

If you want applause just for yourself, turn to the group and say, "Thank you." Unless they are complete dolts, they will applaud.

If you think this is too much like begging, end the trick with some statement that makes it totally obvious that you're done. With the above trick, for instance, you could say dramatically, "So, as you can see, dimes like to be with their fellow dimes, and pennies like to be with their fellow pennies." How do you make it dramatic? Make it a bit louder, and a bit slower. And pause briefly after you say pennies for the first time. You can even hammer the ending home by giving a little nod or a miniature bow.

Illus. 31

Note

At the end, you have a penny finger-palmed in your right hand and a dime in your semi-closed left hand. If the ending described above strikes you as too difficult, try this: Put your right hand over the left and shake the two coins together (Illus. 31). At the same time, say, "Let's see what we have left."

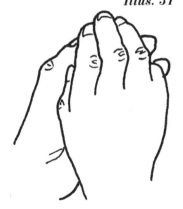

Lift up the right hand. "Good. A penny and a dime."
Proceed as described above.

Coins Across

Coins leap one by one from one hand to the other. This is a
very old trick, and countless methods have been devised over
the years. How does a trick last that long? Only one reason:
It works, and works well. Stupid tricks don't last. And this
one is far from stupid. It looks as though it's real magic. In
fact, it's one that audiences really remember.

One little problem: It takes nerve, and it takes practice.
I'll explain about the nerve later.

First, your audience must be *in front* of you. The final
move of the routine may be revealed if folks are sitting paral-
lel to you.

Preparation: You must have seven quarters in your right
pants pocket. You could use other coins, perhaps, but quarters
work best for me, and I assume they might be best for you as
well.

Step One:

Reach into your right pants pocket and palm one of the
quarters. (See "The Palm," page 12.) Grasp the rest of the
coins in the right fingers. Bring them out and toss them onto
the table.

(You may find it easier to palm one   *Illus. 32*
quarter by putting one coin into the right
pants pocket and the other six into the
left. You stick both hands into the pockets, searching for the quarters. Try it
both ways to see what works for you.)

With both hands spread the coins
out on the table, putting three in a column on the left and three in a column
on the right (Illus. 32).

"This is called the One-Two-Three Trick, and you'll soon see why."

With your right fingers, pick up one of the coins on the left and toss it into your left hand. Pick up another coin with the right fingers and also toss it into your left hand. At the same time, release the palmed quarter so that two quarters land in your cupped left hand. Pick up the last coin on the left with your right fingers. Toss this into your left hand, close the hand loosely, and turn it palm-down.

With your right hand, pick up a coin on the right. Let the coin drop as described in "The Finger Palm," on page 26. It's not quite a finger palm, however; the coin is not gripped, but held loosely as it rests on the third and fourth fingers.

One by one, with the right hand, pick up the last two coins. These two are held by the thumb and the first two fingers. (Now don't get nervous; no one will notice that two of the coins are held differently than the first coin. Honest.)

Illus. 33

Hold the two hands, palm-down, about 10 to 12 inches apart. Raise the hands up and down three times as you count aloud, "One, two, three."

Move your hands toward you along the table as you drop, in a line, four coins from your left hand and two from your right hand (Illus. 33). The extra coin remains in its loose finger palm in your right hand.

Step Two:

With your right hand, pick up one of the four coins from the left side and put it into the left hand. Repeat. Repeat, only this time also release the coin hidden in your right hand, tossing in two at the same time. Pick up the fourth coin and toss it in with the others. Close the hand loosely, and turn it palm-down.

With your right hand, pick up a coin on the right. Let the coin drop into a semi-finger palm, as described above. Pick up the other coin on the right, holding it between the first two fingers and the thumb.

Illus. 34

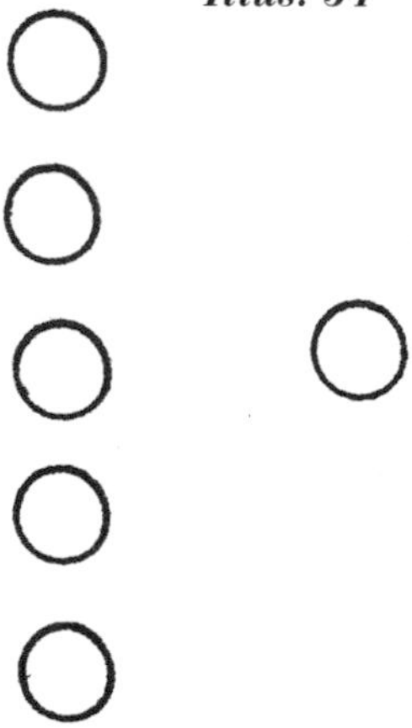

Holding the hands palm-down, perform the One-Two-Three Trick, moving the hands up and down for each digit.

Once more, move your hands toward you along the table, dropping five coins from the left hand and one from the right (Illus. 34). The extra coin is in a loose finger palm in your right hand.

Step Three:

With your right hand, pick up the coins on the left one by one, placing them into the left hand. On the second-last quarter (the fourth you pick up), also toss in the finger-palmed coin from your right hand.

Pick up the coin on the right with your right hand.

Now comes the problem: You already have six coins in the left hand, but how do you get rid of the extra quarter in your right hand?

In my book *World's Best Coin Tricks* is a trick called "Vanish into Thin Air." When I first started doing "Coins Across," I used the latter part of this trick to dump the unwanted quarter. I still do it, because it still works.

Both hands are palm-up and held in a loose fist. You are now going to perform a three-count vanish. But no one will know that it's actually a vanish.

(1) Turn your right side toward the audience. Slap your right hand against the right side of your leg at about knee level. Shout out, "One!"

(2) Turn your left side toward the audience. Slap your left hand *twice* against the side of your leg, also at about the knee. Count off each slap aloud: "One, two!" At the same time as you do the slapping and shouting, drop the coin from your right hand into your right jacket pocket. If you're not wearing a jacket, drop the quarter into your right pants pocket. Close the right hand into a loose fist again.

Illus. 35

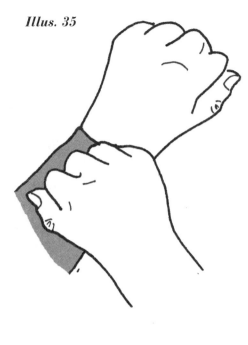

(3) Turn and face the front. Tap the back of the left wrist three times. Tap a little below the hand (Illus. 35). As you make each tap, count aloud, "One, two, three!"

Separate the two hands. Turn them palm-down. Move your hands toward you along the table, dropping six coins from the left hand and none from the right. Let everyone get a good look.

Finally, you might toss in a casual remark: "Easy as one, two, three."

Notes

(1) It's just possible that you're not enamored of that last move. This would be particularly true if you're performing the trick while seated at a table. There's an easy way out.

Take the last coin into your right hand, saying, "I'm going to make it impossible for this quarter to join the others." Stick it into your pocket. Remove the right hand from your pocket, forming it into a loose fist. As described above, tap the back of the left wrist three times, saying, "One, two, three!"

Turn the right hand over, showing that it's empty. Spread the six coins out with your left hand.

"I'll be darned, it *still* got away."

This works because spectators feel that you may have actually retained the coin in your right hand and then some-how sneaked it into the left hand.

(2) This may well become your favorite trick. Practice it for a while. Then try it out on a trusted friend or relative—your sister Barbara, for instance. Chances are you'll be shocked that she's totally fooled. *Do not tell her how you did it, and don't perform it for her again.*

(3) Why are you surprised that the trick worked? Because you're quite sure that every time you added the coin to your left hand, it made a different sound than when you added just one coin. And surely she must know that you're hiding a coin in a finger palm. *Please!* Don't assume that because *you* know something, everyone else must know it too. If the coins make a different sound when you toss in an extra one, no one ever notices. And why in the world would anyone in the group know anything whatsoever about palming coins?

(4) As far as the palm goes, you must, at a conscious level, forget that the coin is there. Use the hand naturally. An inner instinct will make you aware that you can't turn the hand over, revealing the hidden coin.

(5) Relax. Don't be apprehensive.

(6) Perform the trick snappily. Let everyone see what's going on, but don't dawdle.

The Gathering

How about another classic coin routine? The requirements: two playing cards and four coins. The coins are placed in four corners. They are covered in turn by the two cards. One by one, they magically gather under one playing card.

Sometimes a variation will call for four playing cards. And, in some versions—practiced by experts only—the coins suddenly return to the four corners.

Whatever the version, the magician must be able to sneak away a coin and card together. This card and coin are taken away, while another card is set down in the same spot, presumably covering the coin. The card, with the coin hidden beneath, is placed on top of another coin. The two coins now lie separately under the card. Spectators assume that one coin is in each corner. Actually, one card has no coin beneath it, and the other card has two coins beneath it.

The essential move, of course, is sneaking away the coin. I've devised three different methods. In many ways, this is the simplest. The other two methods appear here separately as "A Variation" and "Another Variation."

Requirements: Four quarters, two poker-sized playing cards (somewhat larger than bridge-sized), and three strips of double-stick tape, each about an inch-and-a-half long. (The tape should be transparent. Scotch makes an excellent brand called "Double Stick Tape.") Take one of the two cards and put the three strips of double-backed tape on the face. Illus. 36 shows the position of the strips; they are colored here for clarity, but they are, in fact, virtually invisible.

You're ready now to perform the trick. In this version, you must be sit-

Illus. 36

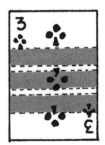

Illus. 37

ting at a table. Later, I'll offer a method that you can perform standing.

Lay out the four quarters in a square; they should be about eight inches apart.

Hold the two cards facedown, one in each hand (Illus. 37). As you can see, each card is held at the side. The taped card should be in your left hand. Place the card in your *right* hand on top of the coin on the upper left. The card is placed directly on the coin. Tap it a few times in the middle with the first finger of your right hand, saying, "Here we cover one coin with one card. And it must be obvious that we can cover the cards any way at all. For instance, we can cover this coin with two cards."

Illus. 38

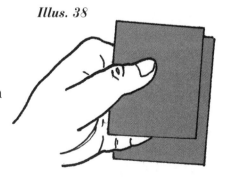

With your left hand, place its card on top of the other. In this instance, retain your grip on the taped card (Illus. 38). The cards do not actually touch except at the front edge.

Reach down and grab

the bottom card in your right hand.
Slide the card to the right, letting it
cover the forward coin there. Let go of
the card.

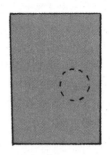

Meanwhile, the left hand continues
to hold the taped card above the coin on
the upper left.

"Or we can cover two coins
separately."

Pause briefly. Lift the taped card.
Bring it down to the coin in the lower left corner.

Place it on top of the coin, so that the coin is at the cen-
ter-right position (Illus. 39). It is especially important that the
coin be centered from top to bottom, so that as much tape as
possible rests on it.

"As you can see..." Rest your right fingers on top of the
card in the lower left position, making sure that the coin will
properly stick. "...we have one card here..." Point to the card
at the upper right position. "...and one card here. All sorts of
variety are possible."

With your right hand pick up the card in the upper right
corner. Place it on top of the card in the lower left corner,
retaining your grip on it. As before, the cards touch only at
the front end.

"We could have *two* cards here, or..."

With your left hand pick up the lower, taped card by the
left side. The quarter, of course, is attached to the bottom.
Draw the card to the left until it clears the card in the right
hand. Let the card in your right hand drop. Move your right
hand away.

"...we could have one card here and one card up here."

Bring the card in your left hand up to the upper left coin.
Place it on top of the coin, making sure that the coins don't

touch (Illus. 40). As you can see from the illustration, the coin that is not attached to the card should be covered by the lower left portion of the card. You don't want both coins to be stuck onto the card. Move your left hand away, letting it drop to your lap.

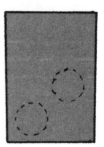

With your right first finger, point to the coin in the lower right corner. "This poor coin never got covered at all. So we must try something special with it."

Pick up the coin in your right hand and take it under the table. As you lean forward, the left arm also goes under the table slightly. So, as the right hand passes by, it slips the coin into the left hand. Continue the forward movement of your right hand. Tap your right fingernails against the underside of the table, as though you're tapping the coin there. "Let's see what happened."

Immediately bring your right hand out. Turn it palm-up as you reach for the card in the upper left corner. Grasp the card

Illus. 41

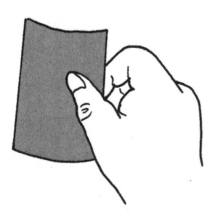

on the right side, thumb on top, fingers below. Bend the right side upward, making sure the stuck quarter gets dislodged (Illus. 41). In the same motion, pick the card up and place it in the left hand, slightly below table level.

All attention is on the two coins as you remove the card, so no one will notice what you're doing as you say, "Two quarters! Very good. It came *up* through the table."

(Now, about that quarter in your left hand. With your hand palm-down and loosely cupped, you've let the coin rest on the tips of your middle fingers. As described above, the right hand brings the card backwards. Your left hand, which is palm-up, lightly grips the coin and card together. Illus. 42 shows the view from below. Note that the coin is held just by the fingertips so that when you place it and the card down, the coin can be easily released.)

Illus. 42

No attention should be on the card you're holding in your left hand because, with your right hand, you pick up the two coins that have been revealed.

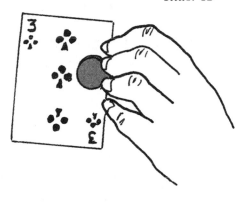

"Two coins," you say, rattling them together.

As you say this, place the card, along with the coin beneath it, onto the table in the upper left position. You might snap the card slightly to make the placement easier and look even more natural.

Transfer the two coins from the right hand to the top of the card.

The current situation: The card in the upper left corner has one quarter beneath it and two coins on top.

The card in the lower left corner has no coin under it, though the group should think that there is a quarter beneath it.

There is a quarter in the upper right corner.

There is nothing in the lower right corner.

Your left hand is slightly below the table. Your right hand picks up the coin on the upper right.

You now repeat the routine you did in apparently knocking a coin up through the table. This time, when you bring your right hand from beneath the table, you bring it palm-up to the card at the upper left position. Grasp the card on the right side. Tilt the two coins off. Move the card aside, showing that another quarter has been pushed up through the table.

"Three quarters! Another one passed right through the table."

Put the card into the left hand, as before. Bring the right hand forward, pick up the three quarters, and give them a shake. Bring the left hand up to the upper left corner. Set the card down with the coin beneath it. Drop the three coins from your right hand on top of the card.

"Let's try something even more difficult. We'll knock a coin *down* through the table and then *up* through the table."

With your left hand, rap a few times on top of the card in the lower left corner. Move the card aside with your left hand, showing that the coin is gone. With your right hand, grasp the card that's in the upper left corner. Flip the three coins off the card. Move the card aside, showing that all four coins are now gathered together.

Work on the trick; you'll love it.

Note

You have put three strips of two-sided tape on the face of a card. But how do you transport this card and the rest of the paraphernalia? I suggest that you use an empty card box. Put in the taped card back to back with another card. Toss in the four quarters. There is little likelihood that the taped card will stick to anything. Close the card box.

You're all set.

A Variation

To perform "The Gathering," you must be seated. How about trying the same trick standing up? It's considerably more challenging, but worth the trouble *if* you have the nerve. I'll make the explanation as brief as I can.

Arrange that two coins be under the card at the upper left, using the card with the two-sided tape, just as before. Pick up either of the exposed coins. Apparently put it into your left hand. Actually, you perform the vanish described in "The Thumb Palm," page 14, or any other suitable vanish.

Aim your left hand at the card in the upper left corner. Suddenly open the fingers in a forward gesture toward that card (Illus. 43). Lift up the card with your left hand, and place it into your right hand, covering the coin.

With your left hand, pick up the two coins on the table. Rattle them as your right hand places the card and coin together onto the table in the upper left corner.

Pick up the other exposed coin in your right hand. Perform the sleight. Complete the routine, as just described.

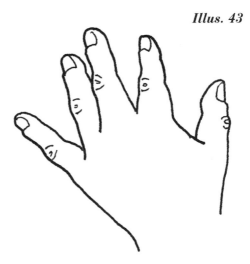

Illus. 43

Finally, you have a coin under the card on the upper left, and three coins on top.

Say, "And now one more magical gesture." Make the dramatic motion with your right hand toward the card on the upper left. Your right hand tilts the card, spilling off the three coins. Finally, move the card aside, showing the fourth quarter.

Another Variation

This version has some advantages. The trick can be done either standing or sitting down. No taped card is used. And you can either knock the coins up through the table, as in "The Gathering," or you can use the sleight-of-hand method suggested in "A Variation."

The cards are held differently than in either of the other versions. They are held at the back with the fingers on top and the thumb below (Illus. 44). This way of holding the cards is essential for the trick move.

Illus. 44

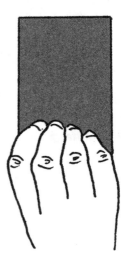

As with the versions described above, hold the two cards facedown, one in each hand. Place the card in your right hand on top of the coin on the upper left. *Retain your grip on the card.*

In effect, say, "We can cover one coin with one card."

Put the card in your left hand on top of the card you're holding in your right hand. Again, retain your grip on the card.

Say something like, "We can cover one coin with two cards."

Slide the bottom card to the right, covering the card in the right forward position, still maintaining your grip.

"Or we can cover two coins separately."

Slide the card on the upper left down to the card on the

lower left. Cover the coin with the card, retaining your grip (Illus. 45). Note that the coin is near the bottom edge of the card, near the thumb.

"We can cover two coins like this."

With your right hand, bring the card from the upper right corner to the lower left corner, and cover the card there. Your grip on the card is retained.

It is important that you be positioned so that your right arm comes directly behind the two cards at the lower left corner (Illus. 46). This guarantees complete concealment as you perform the secret move I'm about to describe.

Illus. 45

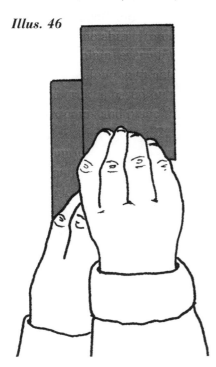

Illus. 46

You are gripping the lower card with your left hand. Lower the back of the card so that it rests right on the coin, but keep your grip. Your thumb is touching the quarter, and the card is bent upward slightly. The fingers are pressing down on the card. It is no great trick then to move the card and coin to the left a few inches and slide them upward.

67

As soon as the lower card clears, *drop* the card held in your right hand. Presumably, it now covers the coin in the lower left corner. With the right hand, reach up and pick up the quarter at the upper left. The left hand continues its upward movement with the card and coin. It stops, leaving the card and coin at the upper left position.

You're holding the quarter that was there in your right hand. Perform the sleight described in "A Variation." Follow the precise procedure in "A Variation," except that you must vanish a coin one extra time.

That's it. Transfer the four coins one at a time to beneath the card at the upper left. As I mentioned, you can use sleight of hand or bring the coins up one at a time from beneath the table.

Under the Table

This absurdly easy effect is most deceptive. Hold any coin in your right hand. It should be resting on your fingers (Illus. 47). Toss the coin into your left hand, immediately closing the left fingers (Illus. 48).

Illus. 47

Illus. 48

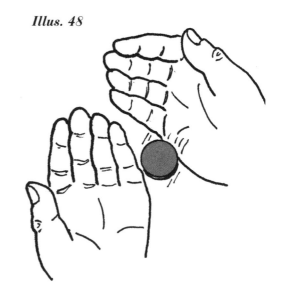

Open the left hand, showing the coin. Don't make a big deal of it; simply show that it's there. In precisely the same manner, toss the coin back to the right hand. Open the hand, showing the coin.

Illus. 49

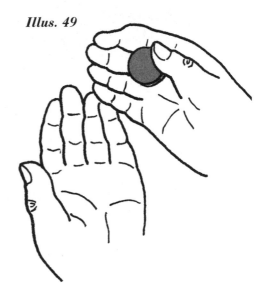

Move the right hand toward the left, duplicating the original motion. The difference is this: As the right hand is turned over, you secure the coin with your right thumb (Illus. 49). Then you duplicate the tossing motion, closing the fingers of the left hand. Immediately slap the left hand onto the table, opening the fingers as the palm is about to make contact.

At the same time, the right hand goes under the table. Turn the left hand palm-up, showing that the coin is gone. Bring the right hand out from under the table, revealing that the coin has passed right through the wood.

Note

The key to the move is the motion of the right thumb. When the coin is first tossed, the thumb should be beneath the hand. This is so that the later grip of the thumb will not be apparent.

More than most tricks, the timing on this one must be perfect. The original two tosses must be matched precisely by the third toss. Practice both ways a number of times. Then check both ways in the mirror to make sure the tosses are identical.

Balancing Act

A penny is balanced on the first finger of the right hand (Illus. 50). The coin is slapped into the open palm of the left hand. Then, quick as a wink, the coin is returned to its original position.

Too good to be true? Of course. And it *isn't* true. It's just a slick trick.

This is a mighty effective little stunt, *but* it requires some practice to get the timing down perfectly. Once you've mastered it, you'll never have to practice it again.

Start by balancing the coin as described above. Turn your hand over so that it's palm-down. As you do so, fold in the first finger and extend the *second* finger (Illus. 51). The penny is held between the thumb and first finger.

Illus. 50

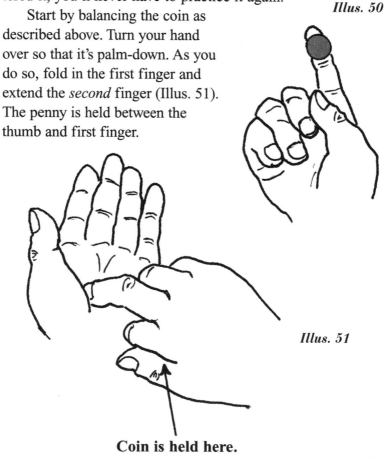

Illus. 51

Coin is held here.

All of this takes place *instantly*. The second finger hits the palm of the left hand. But it's not left there for long. It bounces off the palm, as the hand quickly returns to its original position.

This immediate return to the starting position is *the key move in the trick*. Basically, this is the part that requires practice. Keep at it until the entire series is done quickly and effortlessly.

Repeat the action once or twice. It's quite deceptive, but not deceptive enough to be performed more than three times.

Double Snapper

In my book *World's Best Coin Tricks*, I describe a gag shown me by magic master Milt Kort. He has since developed a wonderful follow-up move, which makes the stunt doubly amusing.

You can use any of the vanishes described earlier. The only proviso is this: After pretending to place the coin into the left hand, you must lower the right hand so that the coin will drop onto your fingers.

Here's the stunt:

When you're paying for a purchase with a coin, show the coin in your right hand, perform the sleight, and slap your left hand on the counter in front of the clerk. At the exact instant that your hand slaps the counter, hit the counter in front of you with the coin in your right hand. The illusion is perfect. Lift your left hand, showing that the coin is not there; then lift your right hand, showing that you still have the coin.

"Just kidding," you say apologetically. Put your right hand on the counter above the coin (Illus. 52). Slide the right hand forward, leaving the coin where it is. As the hand moves forward, your extended arm stays above the coin, hiding its appearance. When you have slid your hand along the counter to the clerk, say, "Here."

Illus. 52

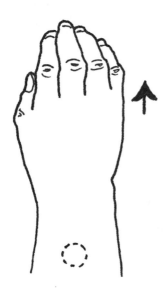

Pause a moment. Then lift your hand, showing that the coin isn't there. Pause briefly. Move your arm aside, showing the coin. With your fingertips, slide it over to the clerk.

I would avoid trying this stunt with burly male clerks who seem surly.

Diving Dimes

Bob Hess developed a highly unusual trick that is quite impressive. And no skill is required, which makes the trick doubly impressive. When performing, you should be fairly close to your audience.

Preparation: You need two fairly tall glasses. Put a penny in each glass. Moisten the bottom of each glass. Put a dime on the *outside* bottom of each glass. Because of the moisture, the dime will stay there.

In performance, tip the glasses forward slightly as you walk among the group, explaining, "Look inside, ladies and gentlemen, and you'll notice that in each glass we have a penny and a dime."

Return to the front. Put one glass on the table. Hold the second glass above it (Illus. 53).

"Watch carefully, please."

Slap the top of the upper glass. The dime should fall off the bottom and drop into the glass on the table. Lift up the glass on the table; at the same time, set the glass in your hand onto the table. Tilt the glass in your hand forward so

Illus. 53

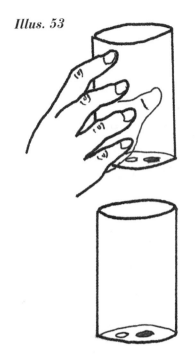

that most can see that a dime has apparently penetrated the bottom of one glass and joined the penny and dime in the other.

"Let's try it again."

You're now holding a glass with a dime attached to the bottom and a dime and a penny inside. On the table is a glass with a penny inside.

Hold the glass in your hand above the glass on the table. Slap the top of the upper glass. The dime should fall off the bottom and into the glass on the table. Hold a glass in each hand. Tilt them forward, showing that each once more contains a dime and a penny.

Note

You set the glasses aside because you don't want spectators to notice the moisture on the bottom. Perhaps they will figure out that the dimes were attached there to begin with. Even worse, they may experiment and match the original condition of the dimes and glasses.

On the other hand, if there is a tablecloth on the table, you can set the glasses down on it at the conclusion of the trick. Gently sliding the glasses forward should eliminate all moisture as you invite the group to examine them.

The bottom line is this: To be completely safe, ditch the glasses when you're done.

Hole Trick

You need a coin (a nickel at the largest), a paper napkin, and a key (or set of keys) in your left front pocket.

Start by cupping your left hand as shown in Illus. 54. Take the napkin into your right hand and spread it over the left hand. With your right first or second finger, poke a little pocket into the napkin (Illus. 55). Squeeze the left hand shut

Illus. 54

Illus. 55

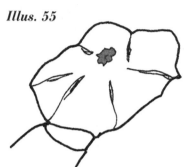

a bit to secure the napkin. This makes it possible for you to poke a hole through the napkin. Presumably, however, you are just making the pocket in the handkerchief a bit deeper.

Pick up the coin in the right hand. Drop it into the pocket in the napkin. Naturally, you let it drop through the hole and into the left hand. The coin should be grasped by the third and fourth fingers as described in "The Finger Palm," page 26.

With the first two fingers of the left hand, squeeze the portion of the handkerchief that forms the pocket. With the right hand, twist the outer portion of the napkin. Pull the napkin from the left hand. Hold it up. It appears that you have twisted the napkin around the coin (Illus. 56).

"Now I'll show you the key

The coin seems to be wrapped up here.

Illus. 56

to magic." As you say this, reach your left hand into your pocket and drop the coin there. Remove the key and hold it up. "Here it is." Tap the napkin with the key; then return it to your pocket.

Tear the napkin up. Start at the hole at the top, tearing straight down. Continue, making sure that the tears obliterate the hole. Hand the pieces to a spectator, inviting an examination.

One-Two

Harvey Rosenthal invented this mystifying quickie.

Start with a fifty-cent piece in each hand (Illus. 57). The coin in the right hand should be in position to make a regular palm. (See "The Palm," page 12.)

Illus. 57

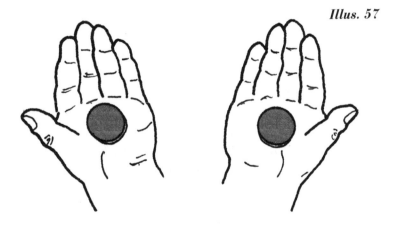

Fold the left second, third, and fourth fingers over the coin in the left hand. With the left first finger, touch the coin in the right hand (Illus. 58). As you do so, say, "One coin."

Reverse the position of the two hands. The coin in your right hand is now gripped in the regular palm. With your right first finger, touch the coin in the left hand, saying, "Two coins." Close the left hand into a fist. You are about to slap

Illus. 58

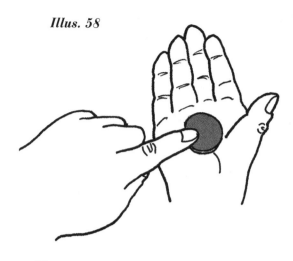

the coin onto the table. As your fist nears the table, open the left hand and slap the coin down beneath it. The coin hits and you say, "One."

Raise the left hand. The coin, of course, remains on the table. Turn the left hand palm-up.

You now perform *exactly* the sleight described in "The Palm," page 12. Briefly, you appear to place the coin from your right hand into the left hand. Actually, you retain it in the palm position in your right hand. The left hand is closed, fingers up.

As you presumably place the coin into the left hand, say, "Two."

Your right hand picks up the coin from the table with the thumb and the tips of the first two fingers. As you pick it up, say, "One." Let the coin rest on the ends of your fingers. The other half-dollar is still palmed in the right hand.

Say, "Two." As you do, let the palmed coin drop on top of the other coin in your right hand, making a clink.

Turn both hands over, showing that the two coins are now together in the right hand.

Something Similar

Let's try a quick, easy trick that is similar in effect to the one just described. In this instance, however, you should work with much smaller coins—pennies or dimes, perhaps.

When I came across this trick some years ago, it was

Illus. 59

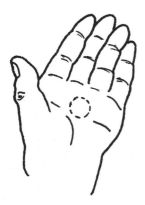

done with matches. Since I never carry matches, I decided to try it out with coins. It worked perfectly. I generally include it in any close-up routine that I do. I think you'll like it; it's not just effective, it's very, very easy.

Let's assume that you're using pennies. Place two pennies onto the table, about a foot apart.

"These two pennies are like some people I know; they just hate to be apart. Watch."

Put your left hand palm-up on top of the penny on the left (Illus. 59). With the right hand pick up the penny on the right, holding it between the first two fingers and the thumb. Once you've picked it up, the penny should be totally concealed from the group by your first two fingers (Illus. 60).

Illus. 60

Push the penny into the palm of the right hand, closing the left fingers onto it as you withdraw the right hand (Illus. 61). As the right hand is withdrawn, the left fingers should scrape lightly against its back.

The left hand

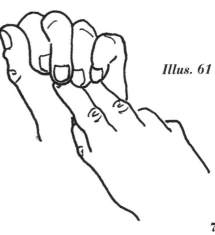

Illus. 61

moves back a little. With the right fingers, you pick up the coin that was under the left hand. The right hand moves several inches to the right. Both hands are now held in loose fists; the left hand is palm-up, the right hand palm-down (Illus. 62).

Illus. 62

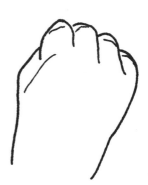

The left hand opens and tosses the penny onto the table in the direction of the right hand. The coin only travels several inches. The right hand turns over and opens, showing the coin it holds.

"See what I mean? The one coin always wants to move close to the other coin."

Nothing magical so far. In fact, this bit is just a buildup for the actual trick.

Place the two pennies a foot apart as you did at the beginning. Put the left hand palm-up on top of the coin on the left. With your right hand, pick up the penny on the right in the same grip as described above. Duplicating the motion you used initially, apparently place the penny into the left hand. Actually, you withdraw the coin as you close up your left fingers.

Move the right hand several inches to the right. Move the left hand toward you, providing the right hand room to pick up the coin. As you move the left hand toward you, extend the first finger of the right hand, closing up the other fingers. This automatically brings

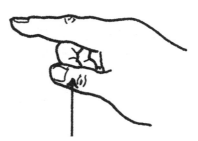

The coin is hidden here.

the hidden coin back, where it is hidden from view (Illus. 63). It also makes it possible for you now to pick up the other coin between your first finger and thumb.

Separate the hands a foot or so. Open the left hand and make a motion as if to roll a coin to the right. But nothing happens. Pause. Open the right hand, showing the two coins. Drop them onto the table.

"They just *have* to be together."

Repeat the trick portion of the routine. Once you've shown that the coins have joined for the second time, call it quits. No use pushing your luck.

Optical Delusion

Seldom, if ever, is an actual magic trick made from an optical illusion. So I'm very proud of my adaptation of this little-known illusion.

First, let's go for the optical illusion. You'll need two coins of the same value. I believe that quarters work best. Pile one of these on top of the other. Hold them flat between the thumb and the first two fingers of the right hand. Slide the top one forward with the first finger as you draw the

lower one back with the thumb. Reverse the movements, sliding the top one back and the lower one forward. If you rapidly repeat these motions, an optical illusion results: It appears that you are holding three coins. Practice this in front of a mirror; you will discover the exact motion required.

Now let's use this illusion in a trick that I devised. In your right-hand pocket, you should have five quarters. Reach into the pocket and grasp one coin in "The Finger Palm" (page 26).

Grasp two more coins with the thumb and first two fingers. Bring the hand forth, making sure no one can see the finger-palmed coin.

"I'd like to show you a peculiar optical illusion." Let all see that you are holding two coins. Take them in the grip described above and perform the sliding motions. "How many coins? It seems to be three, doesn't it?" Stop the motion and hold the two coins up at the fingertips (Illus. 64).

Illus. 64

Ask a spectator to hold out his hand. Drop all three coins into his hand and instantly close up his fingers around them with your left hand. As you do this, say, "I want you to hang on tight to these, so that I won't be able to sneak one away from you."

Reach into your pocket and remove the other two coins, holding them as before. (Make sure that the right third and fourth fingers are closed up, just as they were when you held the extra coin in the finger palm.) *Immediately*, demonstrate the optical illusion, saying, "Here we have two coins." Pause. "But maybe I actually have three coins here." Toss the two coins into your left hand and close the hand into a fist. "I'll con-fess. I *do* have three coins." Open the left hand, showing the two coins there. Look incredulous. "Only two? I could have sworn I had three. What happened to the third one? Would you open your hand, please."

And, of course, the spectator holds the missing third coin.

Going, Going, Gone

In your right pants pocket, you should have a quarter, a fifty-cent piece, and a penny or dime. Let's assume you're using a penny.

Before anyone is aware that you're going to perform another trick, reach into your right pants pocket and remove the quarter, with the penny held flat beneath it. Without call-ing any attention to what you're doing, place the quarter flat on the palm of your left hand with the penny hidden beneath it. Done carefully, there should be no telltale clink.

The left hand should be cupped somewhat so that the penny will not be able to slide out and reveal itself. Hold your hand down so that all can see the coin.

Reach into your pocket once more and remove the fifty-cent piece. Place it on top of the quarter.

Let everyone get a good look.

"Suppose I announce that I'll sell the bottom coin for 15 cents. Would that be a good deal?"

Most will agree.

"Sure. But you should beware of someone offering you a chance to make easy money."

With the right hand, pick up the fifty-cent piece and the quarter together. This is easy to do if you'll dig with your fin-gers beneath the two coins.

Hold out your left hand, showing the penny. Then drop the penny onto the table. At the same time, with your right thumb, slide the quarter away from the fifty-cent piece as you toss the latter onto the table with an inward sweeping motion.

The quarter will naturally be held in "The Finger Palm" (page 26). This leaves the first and second fingers of your right hand free, so it's quite easy to pick up the penny and the fifty-cent piece. After you pick them up, cup your hand and hold it at face level so that no one can see inside. Then jingle the coins, saying, "Easy money can be hard to get."

Return the coins to your pocket.

It Makes Cents

Karl Fulves is well known to magicians. He is an ingenious inventor of magic tricks and a prolific writer in the field of magic. Furthermore, he is an extraordinarily talented publisher, having introduced and edited a number of splendid magic magazines.

Here, he took an ancient principle and applied it to a trick with matches. I've adopted and adapted his idea. I've adopted the basic idea because it's so clever, and I've adapted it to coins.

You'll need a coffee mug you can't see through and approximately twenty coins, preferably pennies.

Start by holding up the coffee mug and saying, "This coffee mug may appear ordinary, but it actually is quite magical. Let me demonstrate."

Toss out all the pennies onto the table.

Tom seems to think he knows how all your tricks are done; it's time to disabuse him. "Tom, I wonder if you'd help me. I'll turn my back and give you some instructions."

Turn to Marie. "And I wonder if you'd do me a favor, Marie. My instructions are somewhat tricky, so I'd like you to help out."

Pick up four coins from those on the table. Drop them into the mug. Pick up the mug and hand it to Marie, saying,

"Would you please hold the magical mug."

Turn your back and deliver these instructions to Tom, with appropriate pauses:

"Tom, I'd like you to pick up a number of coins in your right hand."

"Please take the exact same number into your left hand."

"Let me think for a minute. Got it! Transfer three coins from your left hand to your right hand."

Pause as you ponder your next instruction.

"Oh, let's see. Transfer one coin from your right hand to your left hand."

"Finally, Tom, please give the coins that are in your left hand to Marie. And, Marie, please put the coins into the magical coffee mug."

When they're done, turn around and wave your right hand mystically over the coffee mug. "That ought to do it. The magical mug should make the totals match. Please count the coins in your hand, Tom. Marie, please count the coins in the mug."

They finish and you say, "How many in your hand, Tom?" He tells you. "And, Marie, how many were in the mug?" She tells you. They, of course, announce the same number. "See what I mean? A magical mug!"

Place all the coins into the mug. "Oh, wait a minute! Let's try it again."

Pour the coins from the mug onto the table. As you do so, make sure that *two coins* stay inside the mug. It's easy enough to do this, just don't pour the coins out too rapidly.

Glance at the coins on the table, and say, "There, that's enough." Hand the mug to Marie. Turn your back to the group.

"Tom, please take a certain number of coins into your right hand. Then take the same number into your left hand."

"Transfer three coins from your left hand to your right hand."

Think for a moment.

"I've got it. Transfer *two* coins from your right hand to your left hand."

"Tom, please give the coins that are in your left hand to Marie. And, Marie, please put the coins into the magical mug."

Turn around. Once more wave your hand over the mug. Ask Tom to count the coins he's holding and Marie to count those in the mug.

Once more the number is precisely the same. What a mug!

Note

Suppose you end up with an empty mug or with one coin in the mug when you pour coins out onto the table. Simply correct the count by putting back one or two coins.

Wondrous Flip

This is about as quick as any trick gets. You remove a coin from your pocket—either a fifty-cent piece or a quarter. You show that the coin has a head on both sides.

"Every magician should have a coin like this," you declare. "With a two-headed coin, you could really make money."

Turn to Janice. "Here, Janice, you call in the air."

Flip the coin and catch it. Unless Janice has lost her wits, she'll call heads. Show the coin. "No, sorry, Janice. It's tails."

How in the world did you do that? Well, the "wondrous flip" did not take place when you flipped the coin into the air; it occurred when you showed that the coin had a head on both sides.

When you remove the coin from your pocket, you take it into your right hand and hold it up as in Illus. 65. (Spectators

Illus. 65

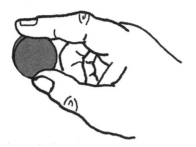

The other side of the coin, which shows a head, is displayed to the group.

see the head on the opposite side.)

"Notice that on this side we have a head." Let everyone get a good look.

Lower your hand and revolve it so that your palm is up. As you make this motion, move your thumb back and up. This push against the coin causes it to flip over. Place the coin on your outstretched left fingers. Illus. 66 shows this, as well as the final position after you have lowered the coin and flipped it over.

"And on *this* side we have a head." As I noted above, say, "Every magician should have a coin like this."

Proceed as indicated above. After you flip the coin, let it land on your right hand. Look at the coin. If it's a tail, perfect. Hold out your hand, showing the coin to Janice. "No, sorry, Janice. It's tails."

If it lands heads-up on

Illus. 66

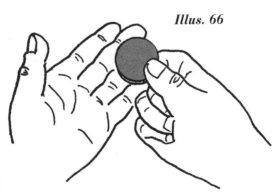

A head can be seen on the upper side of the coin.

your hand, slap the coin onto your left wrist in the traditional fashion. This, of course, turns the coin over. Lift off your right hand and hold out your wrist to Janice so she can see that it's tails. Make the same comment, of course.

Put the coin away. But if anyone wants to see it, there's no reason why it cannot be examined. Needless to say, *don't* repeat the stunt.

—— Bills ——

The Morel Is...

Address the group: "What do we hear about various presidents? You might hear that some are real 'meat and potatoes' kinds of guys. But did you know that our very first president was a mushroom?" Pause. "I'll prove it to you."

Take a dollar bill from your pocket. Make a double fold in the bill—first down and then up (Illus. 67). You're now looking at a mushroom made up of Washington's head and shirt (Illus. 68).

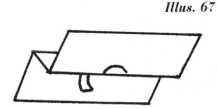

Illus. 67

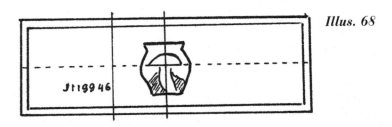

Illus. 68

A Small Amount

Here is a way to fold a dollar bill so that it looks tiny and semi-genuine.

To perform this stunt, you must start by folding a bill exactly as described in the previous trick. Look at Illus. 67 again. Flatten out the bill on a table. Run your thumbnail firmly along the line of the final fold in order to make it lie even flatter.

Basically, only one more combined fold is needed. On

Illus. 69

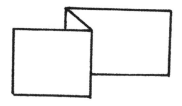

the left side of the bill is a serial number. The points at which you fold the bill are shown by the two lines drawn through the middle of the bill in Illus. 68. The exact method of folding is shown in Illus. 69. Note that both folds must be very sharp.

Illus. 70

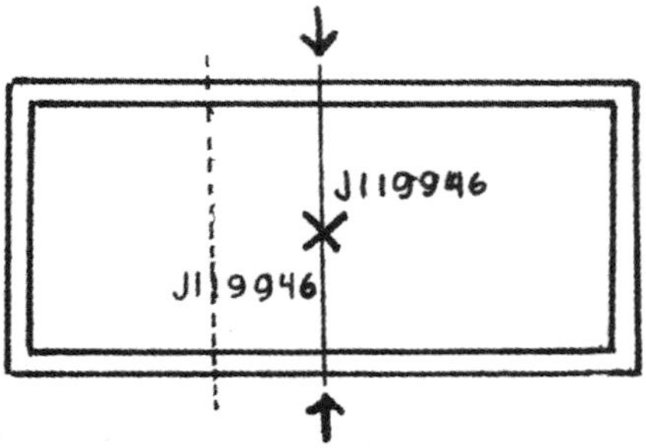

In Illus. 70, you can see that the two serial numbers are on either side of your final fold. The dotted line indicates where the bill is folded underneath. The straight line shows where the fold is made on top.

Again, run your thumbnail along this last double fold to make the bill as flat as possible.

One side looks quite a bit like a miniature bill. *But* it doesn't hang together too well. One way to present the bill is to hold it up with both hands and with your thumb pressed firmly in the exact center. The point at which the thumb would go is indicated by an X in Illus. 70.

As you hold the bill, remark, "I happen to have a little money with me."

Give the group just long enough to catch on to your witty remark, and then snap the bill open.

"Ah, that's more like it. *This* you could spend."

People are surprised when you perform this stunt, but they are not exactly fooled. For best results, put the dollar bill back into your pocket and proceed with another trick or stunt.

Notes

(1) Another possibility for holding the tiny bill together is to use two small paper clips. Stick one on the top and one on the bottom. In Illus. 70, you'll note the two arrows that indicate where the paper clips should go.

With this method, you must remove at least one of the clips before snapping the bill out. This pretty much loses the dramatic climax.

(2) After you have folded the bill, store it in the pages of a very thick book. Or, even better, stick it into a book that is one of a set sitting side by side on a shelf. After a performance, you should refold the bill and store it in exactly the same way.

(3) It wouldn't hurt to prepare two or three bills and store them so that you'll always have some on hand.

Money Roll

Display a dollar bill.

Illus. 71

"An ordinary one-dollar bill," you explain for those with vision problems. "I guarantee you that I can make a five out of this one."

Start rolling the bill at one *corner*, aiming to roll it into a tight spiral (Illus. 71). As you begin, repeat, "I can make a five out of this one."

When you finish rolling the bill up, pull the ends out slightly so that it's close to six inches long (Illus. 72). Then bend

Illus. 72

the bill so that it forms the number five (Illus. 73).

Hold up the number. "There you are—a five out of the one."

Note

Illus. 73

The five you make is not going to look too fancy. In fact, when you display it for the group's inspection, you'll need to grip it with both hands, one on top and one on the bottom.

The Rip-Off

If you'd like to appall persons, you might enjoy tearing up a twenty-dollar bill. It doesn't have to be a twenty; any value will do. You don't *really* tear it up, of course, but you do create a mighty convincing illusion.

Hold the bill as in Illus. 74. Fold about the top half of the bill toward you. As you complete the fold, run your fingernails down the half-bill that is nearer you (Illus. 75). (The illustration shows the right hand at about halfway through its

Illus. 74

Illus. 75

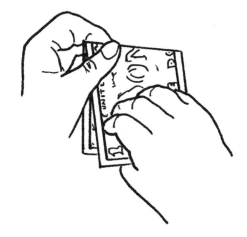

downward motion.) Make sure you press hard with the fingers, and move them downward rapidly. This creates a sound very similar to that of tearing.

Fold about half the remaining bill toward you, and make that same movement with your fingernails, just as though you've torn the bill again.

Do it once again with the small portion remaining.

Stick the "pieces" into your pocket.

If you like to bite your fingernails, you'd better choose a different stunt.

Note
This works much better with a newer bill.

—— Funny Money ——

Up to Date

"Let's try some real magic. I'd like someone to remove a coin from your pocket or purse. Any coin at all. Without looking at it, I'll bet I can tell you the date."

Annie finds a coin in her purse.

"Hold it in your closed hand, and I'll tell you the date."

Dramatically feign concentrating.

"The date is..." Give today's date.

Annie might well say, "But that isn't the date on the coin."

"No, it's the date...today's date. Who in the world could tell you the date on the coin?"

If no one says anything, you can still use the last line.

A Bad Smell

If you like being eccentric now and again, you might like this one.

Carry a really old penny with you, one that looks as though it's been badly mistreated over the years.

When in a jolly group, you might like to address one of the jolliest—Roger. Remove the coin from your pocket and hold it up: "Roger, this is a really weird coin. Do you want it?"

Chances are he'll take it. If not, offer the penny around until someone accepts it. Let's assume that Roger embraces your generous offer.

Hand him the coin, saying, "Now you have this weird coin, Roger." Pause. "In other words, you now have a peculiar scent."

Hearing Test

"Friends, may I suggest that we have a hearing test. June, would you please stop hiding and be good enough to volunteer."

With such encouragement, how could she resist?

Remove from your pocket two good-sized coins—

quarters or half-dollars. "June, I'm going to click these together around your head, and I'd like you to point to where you think the noise is coming from. Easy?"

Of course it is.

"That's really a little too easy. What I'd like you to do is close your eyes to make it a bit more difficult."

She shuts her eyes. Hit the two coins together near her ear. She should identify the direction by pointing.

"Excellent job," you tell her.

You continue to praise her throughout the following.

Try the other ear. The same result.

Try clicking the coins above her head. She points in the proper direction.

But when you click beneath the head in front or near the back of the neck, she will probably miss. Nevertheless, you continue to compliment her.

Eventually, June will notice that the group is chuckling and will open her eyes.

You say to her, "I hate to.............this, June, but you seem..........a real hearing problem."

The dotted lines indicate portions of your speech where you move your mouth but make no noise. The actual sentence would be: "I hate to tell you this, June, but you seem to have a real hearing problem."

Obviously, any other sentence of similar meaning will be just as amusing.

The Glass Refractory

You'll need a fifty-cent piece, a glass of water, and a saucer. The stunt is best performed for just a few persons; they should all be standing. Place the fifty-cent piece onto the table. Directly on top of it, put a glass of water.

"I'd like everyone to step closer and take a look at the half-dollar."

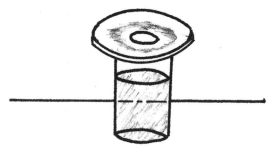

Have the few spectators look *down* at the coin from above the glass.

"Now, with this magical saucer, I'm going to make the fifty-cent piece disappear."

Place the saucer onto the glass (Illus. 76). In most instances, it's impossible to see the coin except from above. Therefore, the coin appears to be gone.

Give the group a chance to look, but don't wait too long before whipping off the saucer, saying, "And now it's back. Gather around and take a look."

Naturally, when the spectators look down, the coin seems to be back. Don't repeat the trick. In fact, it's a good idea to promptly move into your next routine.

Don't Blink

Are you ready to be *really* silly? Take any small object and hold it up for all to see. Let's suppose you are holding a coin.

"Ladies and gentlemen, I am the fastest in the world at making a coin disappear...and then making it reappear. Watch carefully."

Pause for a moment.

"Want to see it again?"

Pay Attention!

I used to love this ancient verbal stunt when I was in the lower grades. My guess is that it's old enough to be unfamiliar to today's citizenry. I came across an excellent version in a well-seasoned book by Gerald Lynton Kaufman.

The basic requirement is that you have acquaintances who are likely to have loose change in their pockets.

"Does anyone have a penny?" you ask.

Someone volunteers a penny. Hold it in your closed left fist. "I'm willing to bet that I have two cents here."

People tend to be suspicious of magicians, so in all likelihood, no one will bet.

Open your hand, showing the single penny. "See? I would have lost."

If someone has the nerve to offer to bet, just open your hand and say, "See? You would have won."

Borrow a nickel from a spectator. Place it in your hand with the penny. Try to make the placement look sneaky.

"I'll bet that I have seven cents in my hand."

Don't really give anyone much of a chance to wager. Open the hand, showing the nickel and penny. "No, just six cents. Once more. This time I'll need a dime *and* a quarter."

Add the two coins to those in your hand. Spread them out so that all can see. Touch the various coins with the first finger of your right hand as you meticulously add them up.

"Forty-one cents, right?"

Very slowly close your left hand. Continue holding it out so that all can see that there are no suspicious moves.

"So you all think I have 41 cents here. I'm willing to bet that I have 42 cents right here in my hand. What do you think of that?"

Pause. "Hey! If I'm wrong, will you let me keep the money?"

Almost certainly, someone will say yes.

"Good. Well, I *am* wrong, so I get to keep the money. Come on...you agreed."

Make sure everyone understands, then add: "Just kidding! I'm not going to keep the money. Why should I? I must have twice this much in the bank."

Falling Down on the Job

The principle involved here is used in many tricks. This handling makes it quite deceptive. *But* you're not going to fool a crowd of persons; you're only going to fool the person for whom you're doing the trick. Practically everyone else will know what you're doing, but will enjoy it all the same.

Any size coin will do; a quarter seems about right. You'll also need a victim. This is not the sort of trick that actually embarrasses someone, so merry, mirthful Melissa would be an ideal choice.

Show her the coin. "Melissa, please hold out your right hand palm-up."

She does.

"On the count of three, I'm going to place this quarter in your hand. You must close your hand up *immediately* so that I can't steal it back, okay?"

She understands perfectly.

Hold the coin in your right hand. Raise the hand to forehead level and then lower it to her open palm. As you come down toward her palm, give a drawn-out, "One!"

Raise your hand up slightly higher and lower it to her palm, saying, "Two!"

Raise your hand to the level of your hair and lower it to her palm, saying, "Three!"

Leave the coin on her palm. If she has understood you correctly, she should immediately snatch the coin and hold it in her fist. If she doesn't, say, "Oh, Melissa, you have to be faster than that. I could have stolen it back easily."

If she does it correctly, compliment her on her swiftness. "Let's try it again," you say. "I want to make sure you can do it perfectly."

In the same way I just described, say, "One! Two! Three!" Each time you raise your hand up a bit higher. Before the last count, you raise your hand a bit higher than before and place the coin on top of your head. You then bring your hand down to Melissa's palm, saying, "Three!" She should instantly close her hand.

Show her that your hand is empty. "Let's see what's in your hand, Melissa." She opens it. Nothing is there, of course.

"What have you done, Melissa? You've lost my quarter! Keep holding your hand out, please. Maybe you can get it back. Just stare at your hand and keep saying magic words to yourself."

After she has stared at her hand a few seconds, tilt your head forward a bit, causing the quarter to drop off your head and into her hand. (You might practice this a bit. It's not particularly difficult. And even if you miss now and then, the coin simply drops to the floor; it's *still* a magical reappearance.)

"Thank goodness you've brought it back, Melissa. You are *really* magical."

—— Bets, Challenges, Puzzles ——

All of these items, dealing with money, are guaranteed to
entertain. You present a challenge to the spectators, which
they will usually fail to solve. You, on the other hand, always
know the solution. The result is that onlookers learn something, and that you are appreciated for your expertise.

Some of these are extremely simple; a few others require
considerable thought. Let's start with the easier ones.

One Too Many

Display a ten-dollar bill.

"How many times does ten—t-e-n—appear on a ten-
dollar bill?"

After the group studies your bill, or perhaps one of their
own, guesses will be made. Most will guess 11.

You point out, "Actually, there are 12. You'll find that
t-e-n occurs in the phrase 'legal tender.'"

Got a Date?

"Can anyone here find the date 1776 on a dollar bill?"

It's possible that someone is astute enough to do so.
Chances to succeed are poor, however.

If no one is able to do it, explain, "You'll find the correct
date at the bottom of the pyramid." If they are still at a loss,
you'll have to point out that 1776 appears in Roman
Numerals: MDCCLXXVI.

Incidentally, older persons will need a magnifying glass
to see it.

Good Old Bill

Your stockbroker friend Josh usually has money on him. Say,
"Josh, I'd like you to take out a dollar bill."

You stand at a goodly distance as you say, "I believe
that's a bill I had the other day. Let's see if I can remember."

Concentrate for a moment. "Yes. I think that the bill has a

7 and a 4 in its serial number. Is that correct, Josh?"

Josh checks his bill. What a coincidence! The bill indeed has a 7 and a 4 in its serial number.

You may want to try it again with someone else. When you do, provide two other digits that you think might be in the serial number. Twice is probably enough. The only time I try a third time is when I've missed on one of the first two. You're unlikely to miss on both numbers, but it's possible. When it happens, say, "Must not be the same bill."

If you miss on just one of the numbers, say, "Well, my mind is drifting, but I at least got one right."

Do I have to tell you? Name any two digits; odds are very much in your favor.

Depends on How You Do It

Hold a small piece of paper—say, three by five inches—in one hand, and hold a quarter or a half-dollar in the other.

"I absolutely believe in the law of gravity," you declare. "Here we have a piece of paper, here we have a half-dollar. I believe that if I drop them from approximately the same height, they will hit the ground at approximately the same time."

Everyone in the group seems to believe that you're wrong. After all, you silly fluff, the lightness of the paper will hold it up in the air while the coin plummets to the floor.

"I can see that you have problems with my proposition. But I can guarantee you that I'm right. The paper and the coin dropped from the same height will hit the floor at almost exactly the same time."

Again, silly objections from the skeptical group.

"If you want me to, I'll be happy to prove it."

Naturally, they'd be delighted to see your idiotic demonstration.

So you demonstrate. Only it's not idiotic; it's just sneaky.

Illus. 77

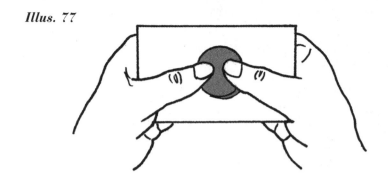

"I will now drop them from about the same height at the same time."

Place the coin *on top* of the paper, at about the middle. Hold it on from both sides (Illus. 77).

Turn the paper and coin loose. They fall to the floor together, landing at about the same time.

Once more the law of gravity triumphs.

Gaffed Bill

In magic, a gaff is the special way an object is fixed in order to accomplish a trick. In this trick, a dollar bill is gaffed.

Search until you find an older dollar bill with the last two digits of the serial number being 19, or something comparable. This is the bill you're going to gaff. You must also find a bill on which the last digit in the serial number is *lower than* the last digit on the bill you're going to gaff. But this digit must also be *higher than* the second-last digit.

So the gaffed bill might have this number at the end: 37.

Eventually you find another bill that has at the end of its serial number 4, 5, or 6. This will be quite satisfactory since the last digit is lower than the final digit in the gaffed bill and is higher than the second-last digit.

How do you gaff the bill? Let's assume that you do have a bill with 37 as the last digits in the serial number, and that the other bill ends in a 5. The dollar bill has two serial numbers on the side where George Washington appears. The one on the left is lower than the one on the right. It is this lower number that you gaff. You erase the last digit of this lower serial number. You can just use the eraser at the end of an ordinary pencil. Considerable rubbing is required, but the digit will eventually be omitted.

The serial number on your gaffed bill now ends in a 3 on the left and ends in a 7 on the right.

To perform the stunt, have both bills in a pocket. Take them out and place them on a table, facedown. Ask Dolores to help you.

"Dolores, in a moment I'd like you to pick up one of those dollar bills and hand it to me. The one you give me will have a higher serial number than the other one. Take your time. Please realize that it doesn't matter. No matter which one you choose to give me, it will have a higher serial number than the other one. If this isn't true, what's the good of being a magician?"

She fearlessly chooses one bill and hands it to you. Glance at the bill. Suppose she has handed you the gaffed bill. Show her the bill, holding your fingers over the lower serial number. Naturally, the higher serial number on the right is displayed.

"What's the last digit, Dolores?"

"Seven," she says.

"Good." Put the bill into your pocket.

"And what's the last digit on your bill?"

She looks it over. "Five."

Shake your head. "I told you."

On the other hand, she may hand you the ordinary bill. If so, set the bill down.

"Let's get dramatic here. Let's see what you kept, Dolores."

Reach over and pick up the gaffed bill. Hold it so that your fingers cover the upper number. Naturally, the gaffed portion is on display. Show it to Dolores.

"What's the last digit, Dolores?"

"Three," she says.

Stick the bill into your pocket. Pick up the one she handed you. Give it to her, saying, "What's the last digit on the one you gave me?"

She looks it over.

"Five," she says.

Shake your head. "I told you."

Note that in either instance, you put the gaffed bill away as soon as possible. You certainly don't want any nosy folk examining the bill.

Note

When you erase the final digit on the gaffed bill, pay no attention to the capital letter that appears at the end. No one will take particular note of the distance between it and the last digit.

A Drop on the Head (or Tail)

You can correctly call whether a quarter will land heads or tails. You will get all sorts of undeserved credit for your great skill.

Illus. 78

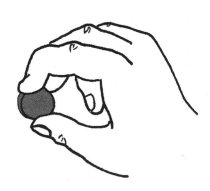

You need a quarter. Hold it in your right hand between your thumb and the second finger. The first finger simply rests on the coin (Illus. 78).

Hold the coin up. "An ordinary quarter. I'm going to drop

it into my other hand. But before that, I'll call heads or tails. And, if all goes well, that's the way the quarter will land."

Call heads or tails.

Hold your left hand about eight inches below the right. Move the second finger of the right hand forward a bit, releasing the coin. The quarter makes one revolution in the air and lands in the left palm. Hold out the palm so that someone can check the coin and note that your call was correct.

How do you make the call? You surely know from the description. As you put the coin into your right hand, look at what is on the upper side. If a head is showing, the coin will land on your left hand as a tail. And vice versa. This is because the coin will make *one* revolution in the air.

Here's why. As you drop the quarter, move your thumb back from it a bit. The quarter ticks against the second finger as it begins its drop; this is what causes it to revolve one time.

Please don't pass this up because it sounds difficult. It's so easy that I'm sure you'll perform it properly the first time.

I suggest that you perform the stunt three or four times. Mix your calls so that spectators won't think that the coin always falls on the same side.

Phony Bet

This quite intriguing effect is the invention of, I believe, Karl Fulves.

Put onto the table a nickel, a dime, and a quarter. Larry loves to participate in all sorts of games, so he's perfect for this trick.

"Larry, how about helping me out."

He'd be happy to.

"Notice that on the table I have a nickel, a dime, and a

quarter. Are you willing to follow my instructions exactly?"

"Sure."

"Good. If you do that, I'll guarantee that you'll hand over to me the highest amount—which is, of course, the quarter. And this is despite the fact that you'll line these three coins up any way you want to."

Larry seems puzzled.

"I'll explain," you say. "Line these three coins up any way you want. Just put them in a row in front of you. They can be in any order at all. But before you do, let me turn away."

Turn your back to Larry.

"Now the idea," you say, "is that you're to follow my directions, and I'll pretty much force you to hand me the quarter. Now line up the coins please—any way you wish."

Pause. Then provide these directions, with appropriate pauses:

"Switch the nickel with the coin to the right of it. If there's no coin to the right of it, just leave the coins alone."

"Switch the quarter with the coin to the left of it. If no coin is to the left of it, just leave the coins alone."

"Switch the dime with the coin to the right of it. If no coin is to the right, just leave the coins alone."

Pause.

"Please hand me the coin on the left."

Turn around and, with hand extended, accept the quarter. Thank Larry for his extreme generosity.

If the group seems receptive, you might repeat the stunt.

The Infernal Triangle

Set out ten pennies, as in Illus. 79.

Say to the group, "As you can see, these coins form a perfect triangle. Can anyone here move just three coins and reverse the triangle? In other words, move three coins and

Illus. 79

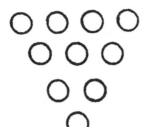

Illus. 80

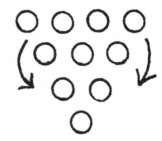

have the triangle face the opposite direction."

How?

First, move the two coins that are in the upper corners. Move them down so that they'll be next to the two coins near the bottom (Illus. 80).

Can you see what you do next? Right. Move the bottom coin up to the top (Illus. 81). The triangle is now reversed.

Illus. 81

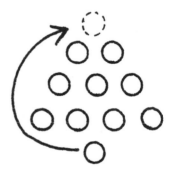

An Easy Move

Line up three pennies onto the table (Illus. 82).

The group has been alert through every trick you've performed, so they just might be ready for a sneaky challenge.

Say to the group, "I have a sneaky challenge for you. Can any of you remove the center coin here without touching it?"

Probably, they cannot.

You, however, in your infinite wisdom are quite bright enough to move one of the end coins to the other end.

Illus. 82

105

Note

A similar trick can be performed with pieces of paper. Place three scraps of paper onto the table in a row.

Say, "Can any of you remove the center piece of paper without touching it?"

If no one else figures it out, you can certainly do it. Simply hold down the two end pieces with your hands and blow the middle piece away.

A Helping Hand

Similar in concept to the trick with scraps of paper mentioned above, this one is quick and easy.

Illus. 83

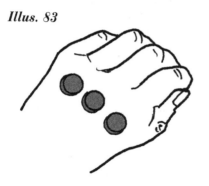

Place three small coins onto the back of your hand (Illus. 83).

"Hard to believe, friends, but I can toss off one or two of these coins. The other coin or coins will remain on my hand. You've all seen me put the coins on my hand, so you know that there's no glue or other sticky substance involved."

Continue to build up the stunt as best you can.

Eileen has been anxious to participate ever since you started. It's time to give her a treat.

"Eileen, I'd like you to pick out one or two of these coins for me to toss off."

Suppose she chooses two coins. With your first finger of the other hand, hold down the coin she has not chosen. With a quick movement of your hand, toss off the other two coins.

If she chooses one coin, hold down the other two with

two of your fingers of the other hand. Again, make a quick movement to dislodge the selected coin.

Clever magic? No. But it's a definite fooler, proving that you can be extremely sly.

A Big Dime!

Toss out some dimes and a fifty-cent piece.

"Question: How many dimes do you think you can place on a fifty-cent piece without any hanging over the edge? And by the way, you can't stack the dimes."

If someone reaches for the coins, say, "No fair until you make a guess."

Chances are excellent that no one will guess the correct answer, which is *one dime.*

A Count for Yourself

You'll need eight coins of the same value; nickels or quarters show up well. Put them in a circle so that they are all heads-up (Illus. 84).

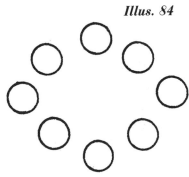

Illus. 84

"I'm going to perform the internationally favorite 'four trick.' After I perform it, let's see if one of you can do it."

Have someone indicate which coin you should start on. Touch that coin, saying, "One." Continue counting aloud up to four as you move clockwise around the circle, touching a coin on each number. When you come to four, turn the coin over.

All the coins are heads-up.

Skip a coin; do the count again. In other words, start with the second coin from the one you just turned over. Again, turn over the coin at the count of four.

Once more, skip a coin, do the count, and turn over the coin at the count of four.

Continue on until all the coins have been turned over. Using this method, you never land on the same coin twice, so—obviously—you always land on a head.

The above explanation is of *what* you do, not of *how* you do it. If you were to proceed directly as described, surely many in the group would figure out how to do it.

How can you be deceptive? Easy. Pause between each move as you puzzle over where you should start next. Move your counting finger around, pausing over different coins before you start on the second coin after the previous turnover.

But here is the trickiest method, one which you should use at least two or three times. After you've turned over the coin, look at the next coin you want to start the count with. Move your counting finger counterclockwise around the circle. Go quite slowly, pausing and moving the finger backward from time to time. Continue the movement until you arrive at your target coin. Start the count there.

After you've finished, let others give it a try. Perhaps they'll get it; perhaps not. You might even repeat the counting yourself.

A Touching Stunt

How about a fairly simple series of moves that spectators will find almost impossible to match? Good.

Lay out six coins as shown in Illus. 85. (I have numbered them to make the explanation as clear as possible.)

Point out the layout to the group. "In three moves, I'm going to place these coins into a circle. Then I'll challenge you to do the same. But there are some rules. First, you must move one coin at a time. Second, each coin that you move must come to rest in contact with two other coins. Third, you must make exactly three moves. And fourth, you must end up with a circle."

Make sure everyone understands.

"Now for my first move."

Take coin number 4 and move it down between 5 and 6. (See Illus. 86.)

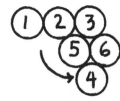

Illus. 85　　　*Illus. 86*

"Notice that the coin is touching two other coins. Ready for my second move?"

Move coin 5 to the left so that it's below and touching 1 and 2. (See Illus. 87.)

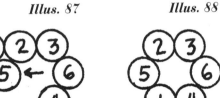

Illus. 87　　　*Illus. 88*

"Again, the coin is touching two other coins. My last move."

Move coin number 1 down to where it's touching coins 4 and 5. (See Illus. 88.)

"There you have it—a circle in three moves. Now it's your turn."

Set the coins up as in Illus. 89. Notice that it's the reverse of the original setup as shown in Illus. 85. Those who remember your first move will most certainly be confused. No one is likely to get it.

Illus. 89

You might give the group another chance. To do so, however, you should pick up the coins and chat for a moment about how difficult the stunt

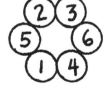

109

is. Then move about a bit so that you lay the coins out in a different spot. Naturally, you use the original layout. After doing the three moves and displaying the circle, pick up the coins once more. Move about a bit before laying out the coins again.

"Maybe you can see them better over here."

Lay out the reverse of the original setup. Perhaps someone will catch on this time. One way or another, don't try your luck a third time.

Instead, try a different stunt. The next one is quite amusing.

Get the Rules Straight

Put three quarters into a row on the table about two inches apart (Illus. 90).

Present this propo-
sition to the assembly:
"These coins look as
though they're an equal
distance apart. But I

Illus. 90

don't think so. Jennie, tell me, which two of these do you think are farthest apart?"

She may estimate that the coin on the right is pretty far from the middle coin. Or she may conclude that the coin on the left is even farther from the middle coin.

Most persons, however, will not guess that the coins on each end are farthest apart.

The Sliding Dime

Hold up a dime. "Here, my friends, is a genuine dime. Believe it or not, I'm about to perform a miracle with this ordinary coin. I'm going to drop this coin from a height of more than four inches, and it will land on edge on the table."

Note the dubious looks. "I promise you, I'll drop the dime from more than four inches, and it will land on its edge."

Wet the sides of a tall, straight glass. Place a dime against the side near the top. The coin will stay there—usually briefly. Sooner or later, however, it will slide down the side to the bottom of the glass, where it will remain standing on edge.

Note

You need not run to the kitchen to wet down a glass. Before you start, set down a glass that's full of water. When ready to prove your statement, reach into the glass with your fingers and get some water, which you rub down the side of the glass. You may have to dip in a few times to get enough water. Try the stunt in advance to see how much will work for you.

Very Odd Man

There is an ancient schoolboy stunt that can make for an entertaining trick. I first worked this routine many years ago and have since discovered that hardly any coin tricks provide as much enjoyment for so little effort.

The original trick was simplicity itself. Let's suppose that three of you decide to "match pennies." Each of you shakes up his penny, and then, simultaneously, all uncover their coins. If all three coins are heads or tails, it's a standoff; you must try again. Otherwise, the "odd man" wins. Who's the odd man? He's the one who has a tail when the other two show heads. Or he has a head when the other two show tails.

If two of the players decide to secretly cooperate, they can cheat the third player. All they have to do is make sure that one shows a head and the other shows a tail. Obviously, whatever side the poor victim shows, he's bound to lose. Later the two sneaks split the profits.

So, what's the fun in two persons victimizing a third? I'm glad you asked. Here it is:

You'll require two assistants. Choose John first. "John, I'd like you to assist me in a gambling demonstration."

When John comes up, hand him a quarter. "I'm only

lending you this quarter, John; I don't have that much money to spare. Now let me tell you what I want you to do."

Turn John away from the group. Remove another quarter from your pocket. Explain quietly: "John, you and I are going to victimize our next volunteer. The three of us are going to match coins." Put the quarter on your left palm (Illus. 91). Suppose it shows a head. Call that to John's attention. Put your cupped right hand on top of the coin (Illus. 92).

Illus. 91

Illus. 92

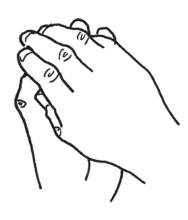

Shake the two hands up and down together, presumably bouncing the coin around. Although the palms are far enough apart to create the illusion that the coin could be turning over, the quarter stays exactly the way it was when you put it into your palm.

Show John that your quarter is still heads. "See that, John? If you shake the coin that way, it'll stay the way it is when you put it down. Try it."

He does.

"We'll match coins with another assistant. Odd person wins. So if you have heads, I'll have tails. And vice versa. Just keep your eye on me. If I touch my head in any way, that means I'm going to show heads. If I don't, that means I'll show tails. Your job is to show the opposite."

Make sure John understands.

"So people won't guess that we're up to something, I'll spend some time with the other volunteer, just as I spent time with you."

Turn back to the group. "This time I'll choose Annette. Would you please come up and help me out, Annette."

Of course she will.

Hand Annette a quarter, explaining that you're poverty-stricken and will definitely need it back. Turn her away from the group. Explain how the three of you will play odd man. Naturally, you don't tell her that the game is rigged. Show her how to bounce the coin between her hands. The difference is that the palms are much farther apart so that the quarter actually does turn over several times.

Turn back to the group. "Now I think they both understand how to match coins. It goes like this: We all shake our quarters. Then we look to see what everyone has. If all three have heads or tails, then it's a draw. But if there are two heads and a tail, or two tails and a head, the person with the odd coin wins. We're going to play a number of times, so I'd like the audience to keep score."

You will now show heads a few times in a row, followed by a tail, and then by another head, a few tails, and so on. You can follow any order you wish. Just remember to mix them up. And don't forget to signal John.

When you're going to show a head, rub your chin, or scratch your ear, or brush back your hair—anything, just so you touch your head. Otherwise, of course, you show a tail.

The point is that Annette *never* wins. After several rounds, ask the audience the score. Suppose you have five wins and John has three. "Annette, are you trying your hardest? Come on now, give it a good shake."

Eventually, the audience and Annette will catch on that

she can never win. At this point, you can simply say, "Gee, Annette, I've never seen such bad luck."

Thank your assistants and call it quits.

This makes for rather a flat ending, I believe. Much better is to explain to the group exactly what you and John have been up to. The climax? After you finish your explanation, say, "How about a nice hand for my partner in crime, John?"

When the din dies down, continue: "And how about a special hand for a very good sport—Annette!"

As I say, an easy routine that's lots of fun for everyone.

Under the Cap

Needed: Two quarters, a bottle cap, and an attentive audience. The bottle cap should be the size that comes on a 20-ounce cola. A quarter can easily fit inside.

"Let me tell you a story about a swindler and a bottle cap." Hold the cap up so that all can see it. "The swindler was a street gambler, who set up his table in the midst of a crowd. He took out a quarter..." Remove a quarter from your pocket. "...and said to the group, 'Ladies and gentlemen, I'd like someone to take this quarter and shake it up. I'll look away while this person places the quarter under the cap. I guarantee that I can tell whether the quarter is heads or tails without sneaking a look under the cap. Are there any bets?'"

"Actually, he did get some bets. 'Put your bets on the table,' said the swindler. And some of the people did. Then, while he looked away, someone shook up the quarter, put it onto the table, and put the cap on top of it.

"The swindler turned his head completely away as he had a little coughing jag."

Turn aside and do some coughing into your hand.

"A wise guy winked at the group, lifted up the cap, and took the quarter."

Take the quarter from under the cap and set it aside.

"The swindler turned back to the group and said, 'Now I must decide whether the quarter is heads or tails. If I get it right, I win the money; if not, the betters win. Let me see.'"

Tap the top of the bottle cap thoughtfully.

"The swindler said, 'I'll say that the quarter is heads.' One of the group turned the cap over, laughing."

Lift off the cap.

"But he didn't laugh for long. As you can see, the coin was heads."

(I'll explain how you do this below.)

Sit down at the table.

The situation: Two quarters are on the table. The cap is also on the table.

Pick up the two quarters with your right hand. Presumably put them into your pocket. Actually, put just one into your pocket. Retain the other in "The Finger Palm" (page 26). Let the right hand, holding the coin, drop into your lap.

While doing the following, drop the quarter from your right hand so that it lands under the table onto the carpet. With the left hand, pick up the bottle cap. Meticulously show it inside and out. Set it onto the table, open side down.

"In a moment, very magically, I will make a quarter appear under the bottle cap."

Make some mystical waves over the cap. And toss in some semi-magical words if you'd like to build suspense.

"I'm done." Nod your head to a spectator. That person will turn over the cap. Naturally, there is no coin on the table.

"What did I promise you? I said that the quarter will be under the bottle cap, right?"

Right.

"What's under the table? The carpet, of course. And what's on the carpet?"

Push your chair back and point to the quarter that's on the floor under the table.

"There's the quarter. And, as I promised, it's *under* the bottle cap."

Note

Wonderful! But how do you do the first part of the trick? Simple. Take a little bit of double-stick tape and put it inside the bottle cap. Place a quarter inside the bottle cap and press it *firmly* against the tape. You should probably hold it there for several seconds to make sure that it sticks. But then it can't stick too much, or it won't drop out when you want it to.

When you act as the spectator who removes the coin, replace the cap on the table with a little smack to dislodge the quarter. If that doesn't seem to work, tap the cap as you contemplate whether it's heads or tails.

Make sure that there is a cloth of some sort on the table. You don't want the quarter to make a telltale noise when it hits the table.

Incidentally, make sure the quarter hidden in the cap is turned properly to show the side that you predict.

Two in a Row

You'll need eight pennies and eight dimes for this sneaky puzzle. Lay them out as shown in Illus. 93 (the dark ones are pennies).

Tell the group: "I have an extremely difficult puzzle for you. Here you see that I have a mix-ture of dimes and pennies. The question is this: Can you arrange it so that you have all dimes in two of the rows and all pennies in two of the rows? Nothing to it, right? Well, there's one little problem: You're only allowed to *touch* two coins."

Illus. 93

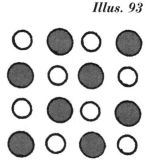

Illus. 94

Illus. 95

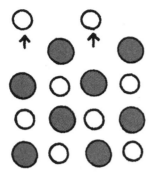

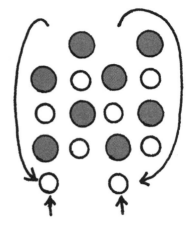

Chances are excellent that no one else can figure it out. You, however, with your magnificent brain can perform the stunt with ease.

Illus. 96

With the first finger of both hands, move two dimes up, as indicated in Illus. 94.

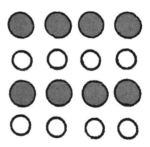

Move them around on each side to beneath the formation, placing them beneath the pennies at the bottom (Illus. 95).

Push the two dimes upward against the pennies, moving the entire column upward one position. The pennies and the dimes are now all in a row (Illus. 96).

An Old Turkey

Perhaps you've heard the song, "Everything Old Is New Again." In the field of magic, I don't know about "everything," but a great many old tricks are still extremely effective. And old puzzles can still befuddle.

On the middle of a sheet of paper, trace with a pencil the outline of a dime. Fold the paper across the middle of the outline

Illus. 97

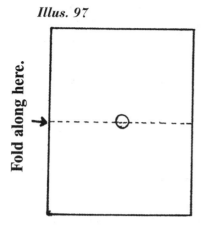

Fold along here.

(Illus. 97). Take a scissors and cut out the portion marked with a pencil (Illus. 98). Result: a hole the size of a dime in the middle of the paper.

Ready? Take out a quarter and address your friends: "Is anyone here really magical? To put it another way, can anyone here drop this quarter through this hole?"

It's really unlikely. Perhaps *you'll* have better luck.

Illus. 98 **Cut here.**

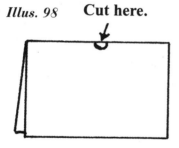

Nothing to it. Just place the quarter in the middle of the paper, on the hole. Take up each corner of the paper and bring them together. Holding them on top, give the paper a good shake. The quarter will fall through the hole.

A Really Old Turkey

You might as well use that hole in the paper again.

"All right, folks, you've seen me do the impossible with a quarter. Now I'm going to try to push a half-dollar through the hole *without enlarging the hole*. Anyone want to try it first?"

Some of your pals may have that old do-or-die spirit, but chances are it won't do them much good. You rogue, you've just fooled them with an old verbal trick.

When they finally surrender, say, "Now I'm going to *push* this half-dollar through the hole. Watch carefully."

Set the half-dollar onto the table. Put your little finger through the hole and jab the half-dollar. You have indeed pushed the half-dollar through the hole. Incidentally, if you have a really fat little finger, you can use a pencil or pen.

—— Routines ——

In my opinion, there is no set routine that can be used on all occasions. Your pattern of coin tricks depends entirely on the circumstances. Obviously, you will perform different tricks for a few friends than for a large group in a formal presentation.

First, let's consider larger groups. As much as possible, try to arrange it so that you face the entire group. In other words, you should face the audience. This is obvious when you're performing a formal show. But it's less apparent when you're performing an impromptu show—in a living room perhaps. When persons are sitting all around, you might suggest that the group gather on one side of the room. "Would you mind? I'd like to act like a real magician."

So let's assume that you're facing a fairly large group. What kinds of coin tricks do you perform?

Start with something fairly mild that will quietly get everyone's attention. For instance, use one of the sleights to pretend you're placing a large coin into the left hand while actually retaining it in the right. Pause. Show that the coin has disappeared from the left hand. Reach out and produce the coin from someone's ear—preferably a child's.

The next trick should be a real grabber, probably your second-best effect. For instance, you might do "A Falling Off" (page 30). (Although the trick calls for the use of a table, it can readily be performed on the floor or carpet.)

In fact, you might decide to do the first three tricks under "Coin Tricks." After doing "A Falling Off," you could also perform "Cross-Up" and "Get Your Teeth into It."

Any number of tricks could follow. You could perform a few interesting quickies, like the unusual spinning coin in "Put a Spin on It" (page 48), or "Balancing Act" (page 70).

What next? Time for another arresting trick—for example, "Optical Delusion" (page 79).

Follow up with something mild—any of those in "Coin Moves" (beginning on page 12) would do.

Next could be a strong trick or two. Close with what you consider your strongest trick. I recommend "Cups and Coins" (page 49).

Suppose you're in the living room and persons are sitting all around. For whatever reason, they don't wish to move to one end; perhaps the group is too large. What sort of trick can you do? A few of those in "Coin Moves" would be appropriate. Play first to one side of the room, and then to the other. Layout tricks would be perfect—for instance, "The Great Escape" (page 35). Another possibility is "Which Way Did They Go?" (page 47).

In this circumstance, you must choose tricks that will not exclude anyone. For example, you can try tricks like "Optical Delusion" (page 79). In this instance, you show all sides of the audience the illusion of two coins as three, and then proceed.

Being encircled, you may decide to show any of the tricks in "Bets, Challenges, Puzzles" (beginning on page 98).

Another possibility: Seated at a table with friends, you're asked to do some tricks. No problem. Let's assume it's a dining-room table. Move to the end of the table and begin your show. Perhaps Joan is seated at the convenient table end. If so, ask her to change seats with you. Now you're ready to perform a variety of tricks suitable for work at a table. Check it out.

Perhaps it's not convenient to perform at the end of the table. Beware! You have persons on all sides. Certain table tricks are still available to you, but not all.

"A Falling Off" (page 30) would work all right, as would the two tricks following it.

Another excellent choice would be "Under the Table"

(page 68). Also a good choice is "One-Two" (page 75). I'm sure you can find others yourself.

But definitely avoid tricks where a lateral view might reveal the method—"Coins Across," for instance.

Suppose you have a small social group in the living room. You'd like to perform some of the classy table tricks. Say to the group, "How about joining me at the table. I'd like to show you a few slick stunts."

An ideal situation? I've always liked a chance to perform when seated at a restaurant with several friends. It's the perfect opportunity to do a few of the tricks described in "Coin Moves." In this happy circumstance, two or three tricks are plenty. Sometimes even one is enough, particularly if your first trick gets an extremely positive response.

After golf, a number of friends and I went to a restaurant to celebrate the fact that we'd completed 18 holes without collapsing. Denny likes extra butter on his toast. Only one pat remained on the table. Fortunately, it lay in front of me.

All attention was on the butter. I picked up the pat with my right hand and pretended to place it in my left hand. I let my right hand drop casually to my lap. Denny reached for the pat. I slapped my left hand on the table and then lifted it up, showing my palm was empty and the pat wasn't there.

"Oops! Too hard," I said.

I pushed my right hand under the table and brought out the pat of butter. No additional patter was necessary. Appreciative comments were offered by all. No further tricks were needed.

Incidentally, impromptu opportunities like this abound. Just be on the lookout for them.

Here's another profitable situation: You're alone on one side of a table, and one or two persons are on the other side. In this situation, you can perform virtually *any* trick.

Here are some general points to remember:

• You make a coin disappear and then reappear again. You have learned several clever ways to do this. But don't do more than one or two at a time. The reason? Observers believe they're seeing the same trick over and over. The coin goes, it comes back. Big deal.

• You can use the disappearance/reappearance as an amusing running gag by performing one here and there between major tricks.

The important thing when building a routine is to provide *variety* in as many ways as you possibly can. Do long tricks, short tricks, serious problems, amusing stunts—just make sure there is a constant change of pace. This makes for better entertainment for both you and your audience.

Some magicians think it's a bad idea to present an entire routine of money tricks. "It's bound to be too dull," they declare.

I don't see why. A routine lasting five to ten minutes can be quite interesting. Mind you, I prefer to mix in other kinds of tricks. For one thing, I can do a longer routine that way. So if you know some other kinds of tricks, consider throwing them in here and there amid your money tricks.

Here is the most important rule of all: Know when to quit. It could be after one trick, or after a dozen. It depends on the group. Have they had enough? After enough experience, you may know just *before* they've had enough. In any instance, it's better to stop too soon rather than too late. If you see interest is dwindling, stop really soon.

I close almost every routine with this: "I'd now like to perform my very best trick." Significant pause. "I'm going to quit while I'm ahead."

— Mastery Levels Chart & Index —

Trick	Page	Easy	Harder	Advanced
Another Vanish	23			☆
Another Variation	66			☆
Bad Smell, A	92	☆		
Balancing Act	70	☆		
Big Dime!, A	107	☆		
Coins Across	54		☆	
Count for Yourself, A	107	☆		
Cross-Up	32		☆	
Cups and Coins	49			☆
Depends on How You Do It	99	☆		
Diving Dimes	72	☆		
Don't Blink	94	☆		
Double Snapper	71	☆		

123

Sterling Books by Bob Longe

Card Tricks Galore
Clever Card Tricks for the Hopelessly Clumsy
Easy Card Tricks
Easy Magic Tricks
Little Giant Book of Card Tricks
Little Giant Encyclopedia of Magic
Magical Math Book
Mind Reading Magic Tricks
Mystifying Card Tricks
Nutty Challenges & Zany Dares
101 Amazing Card Tricks
World's Best Card Tricks
World's Best Coin Tricks
World's Greatest Card Tricks